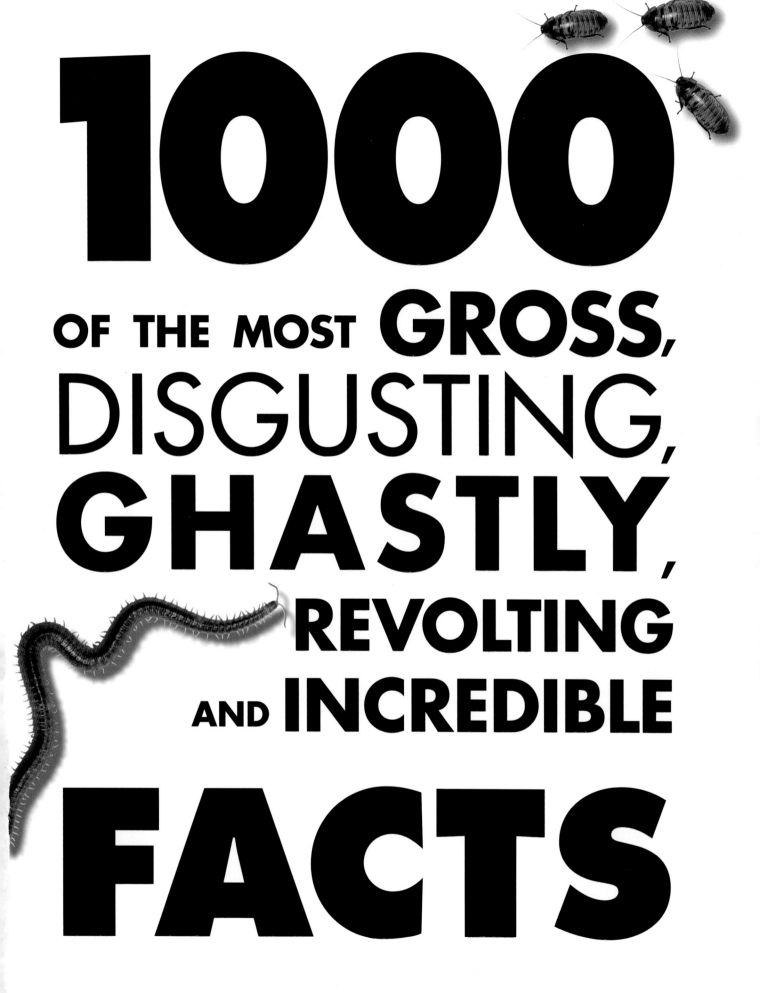

# 1000

## OF THE MOST GROSS, DISGUSTING, GHASTLY, REVOLTING AND INCREDIBLE FACTS

This edition published by Parragon Books Ltd in 2014

Parragon Books Ltd
Chartist House
15–17 Trim Street
Bath BA1 1HA, UK
www.parragon.com

Copyright © Parragon Books Ltd 2014

Designed, produced and packaged by Tall Tree Ltd

ISBN 978-1-4723-7776-0

Printed in China

# 1000

## OF THE MOST GROSS, DISGUSTING, GHASTLY, REVOLTING AND INCREDIBLE FACTS

Bath · New York · Cologne · Melbourne · Delhi
Hong Kong · Shenzhen · Singapore · Amsterdam

# CONTENTS

# 1

# BEASTLY

# BODIES

Most people have **tiny mites** in their eyelashes, **no matter how clean** they are.

#0001

# 11 facts about SLIMY SNOT

The scientific word for nose-picking is **RHINOTILLEXOMANIA.**

#0002

A person **swallows about a litre of snot** a day without even realizing it.

#0003

Snot is made of **water, salt and a gluey, sugary substance called mucin...**

#0004

... When the water dries out it turns into **hard bogies.**

#0005

**Snot** moves through your breathing tubes at **1.5 centimetres per hour.** Bamboo grass grows more quickly than this.

#0006

**A sneeze hurtles out snot at over 60 KILOMETRES PER HOUR –** that's nearly twice as fast as a London tube train. #0007

The world sneezing record is held by British girl Donna Griffiths. She **SNEEZED A MILLION TIMES IN A ROW.** #0008

If you've been hanging out in a **dusty room,** your snot will be a **GREY dust-colour.** #0009

**Your snot** looks more **yellow** when you have **a cold** because of all the **white blood cells** in it. #0010

**YOUR SNOT protects you** from dirt and germs in the air by catching them. #0011

Snot is more than just sticky goo. It contains **antibodies** that help the body recognize **invading bacteria and viruses,** and creates **enzymes** to help kill them. #0012

# 9 SLOBBERY SPIT FACTS

**Your mouth produces between ONE AND TWO LITRES OF SPIT** (also known as saliva) a day.

#0013

**Your saliva turns your food into a SOUP-LIKE MIXTURE,** which makes it easier to swallow.

#0015

Yawning really hard can make your spit spray **more than a metre.** This is called **GLEEKING.**

#0016

In some parts of the world, it is thought that a **mother's saliva can help build up a child's immune system**, so mums chew their baby's food before feeding it to them.

#0014

**In Singapore, you can be fined £1300 for spitting in the street.**

#0017

# A single COW

makes as much **saliva as 200 HUMANS.** It helps them to chew all that grass. #0018

# FULMAR CHICKS SPIT

at other animals to keep them away. #0019

Llamas spit when they get annoyed. Their spit is super smelly because it includes food from their stomach. #0020

Spitting cobras spit painful venom **straight into the eyes of predators,** and then slither away to safety. #0021

11

# 8 EYE GOO FACTS

Your eyes make tears to wash away dirt and **stop your eyeballs drying out**. #0022

When you wake up, there is often a **yellow crusty goo** around your eyes. This is **DRIED-OUT TEARS**. #0023

Your tears contain water, oil and mucus (snot!). #0024 **This makes the tears stick to your eyes.** #0025

WHEN YOU CRY, **some tears come out of your nose.** They run down a passage connecting your eyes and nose. #0027

You blink about **25 times a minute.** #0028

It takes 100 tears to fill a teaspoon. #0026

If your eye gets an infection or becomes too dry, it may start to leak a yellow, green or grey fluid known as pus. #0029

12

# 4 Icky Earwax Facts

Earwax keeps your ears moist, and makes sure that **dirt** and **bugs** can't get in. #0030

In the 19th century, magazines recommended **using earwax as a lip balm.** #0032

Earwax is made from **sweat, body oil and dead skin.** #0031

Inside each blue whale's ear is a **30-cm-long** plug of **earwax**, which protects the eardrum when the whale dives underwater. #0033

13

# 7 STOMACH JUICE facts

Fat is hard to digest. It congeals in large globs in your insides, and you need a **substance called bile** to dissolve it. Without the bile, it would just stay there. #0034

The acid in your stomach is strong enough to **eat through metal.** #0035

When stomach acid leaks into your gullet (food pipe), you get a searing feeling called **HEARTBURN.** #0036

**Spicy and salty food** make your stomach acid even more acidic, which can cause heartburn. #0037

14

Your body makes more than
# SEVEN LITRES
# OF DIGESTIVE JUICES
every day. If you tried to drink that much liquid in one go, it would kill you. #0038

Food needs **three to five hours** to dissolve in your stomach juices before it is ready to go to the small intestine. #0039

**Your stomach is lined with a gooey mucus that digests the food.**
# STOMACH ULCERS
happen when there is a gap in the mucus. #0040

# 3 VILE VOMIT FACTS

Vomit is very **ACIDIC** and dissolves your teeth. #0041

Vomit contains half-digested food and bits of stomach lining, which look like **lumps of carrot.** #0042

When one person vomits, it makes **everyone** around them feel sick, too. This can be useful if you've all eaten something **poisonous.** #0043

16

# 5 PONGY POO FACTS

People **fart 14** times a day. #0045

**1/3** of your **poo** is made of bacteria. #0047

**Cabbage** contains **stinky sulphur**, which gives you **smelly farts.** #0046

# 11 facts about PEE

When it first comes out, pee is **cleaner** than spit. #0049

**urine is 95 per cent water.** #0050

**The other 5 per cent** is old body cells, unwanted material from your food and salt. #0051

**Ancient Egyptian doctors used to taste people's urine to find out if they were diabetic.** #0052

You pee between one and two litres of urine a day. #0053

Some people think **drinking your own pee** makes you healthier. #0054

# Throughout your life, you pee about **45,000** litres of urine. #0055

That's enough to fill a small swimming pool.

**Your pee is yellow because of a chemical called urochrome.** #0056

You can pee faster or slower by controlling the muscles underneath your bladder. #0057

Male lobsters have bladders in their heads, and shoot pee at each other. #0058

If you eat **asparagus,** your pee will smell of it. #0059

# 5 Facts about Burping

Swallowing air as you eat and drink can make you **BURP** and fart. #0060

Burping gets rid of a litre of gas from your **stomach** every day. #0061

Drinking through a straw can **make you burp,** because you swallow more air. #0062

In the zero-gravity of space, **ASTRONAUTS WET BURP** because some of their stomach contents come out, too. #0063

The **LOUDEST BURP** ever recorded was as loud as a **car alarm.** #0064

# 8 BAD BACTERIA FACTS

Lots of bacteria live in your armpits and feet. They live off the sweat. #0065

A single gram of fluid in your large intestine contains 10 trillion bacteria. #0066

There are about 3000 microbes (tiny bacteria) on every square centimetre of a desk. #0067

If you could get bacteria to line up in a row, 10,000 would fit across your fingernail. #0069

A piece of chicken that is starting to smell is covered with at least 10 million bacteria per square centimetre. #0068

Hot water is much better than cold water at getting rid of bacteria from your hands. Most bacteria are frazzled by the heat. #0070

A kitchen sink is home to 10,000 times more germs than a toilet. #0071

One bacterium can turn into millions of bacteria in less than a day. #0072

# 6 DEADLY DISEASE FACTS

More than 220 million people around the world suffer from malaria each year.
#0073

The Black Death killed more than 25 million people across Europe, which was one third of the population at the time.
#0074

The plague germ was spread by rat fleas. It was called Yersinia pestis.
#0075

On average, one person catches tuberculosis every 3.6 seconds.
#0076

There can be as many as 5 billion viruses in one drop of blood.
#0077

Smallpox killed 30 per cent of the people who caught it.
#0078

# 7 SWEATY facts

Sweat is a mixture of water, salt and minerals that **evaporates into the air,** taking body heat with it.

#0079

**If sweat stays on your skin** for a while, bacteria start to eat it, creating the pongy chemicals that make you **smell.**

#0080

24

Dogs hardly sweat at all, and have to hang out their

# TONGUES

to get rid of body heat.

#0081

Hippo sweat is red and sticky, and it acts as

## sunblock. #0082

COWS SWEAT mostly through their noses.

#0084

There are about

# 250,000

sweat glands on one foot.

#0083

**Your feet shed dead skin cells** all day. The skin cells mix with **SWEAT** to make a **smelly goo** that is rolled into a **CHEESE** by your toes.

#0085

25

# 6 FACTS ABOUT BLOOD

The average human has nearly **5 l of blood** in their body – enough to fill five family-sized bottles of fizzy drink.

#0086

Red blood cells are created and **destroyed** at a rate of about **2 million** per second. That's **173 billion** cells per person per day.

#0087

The amount of blood that is pumped through an average human heart every day would fill about

# 85 BATHS.

#0088

When you **CUT YOURSELF**, **13** different **chemicals** work together to turn blood into a **jelly-like** clot. After that, a scab can start to form. #0089

# PUS

**is a gooey** yellow gloop made from dead **white blood cells** that are left over when your body attacks an **infection.**

#0090

# SCABS

**start to form** less than 10 seconds after a cut has opened.

#0091

27

# 15 BRAIN FACTS

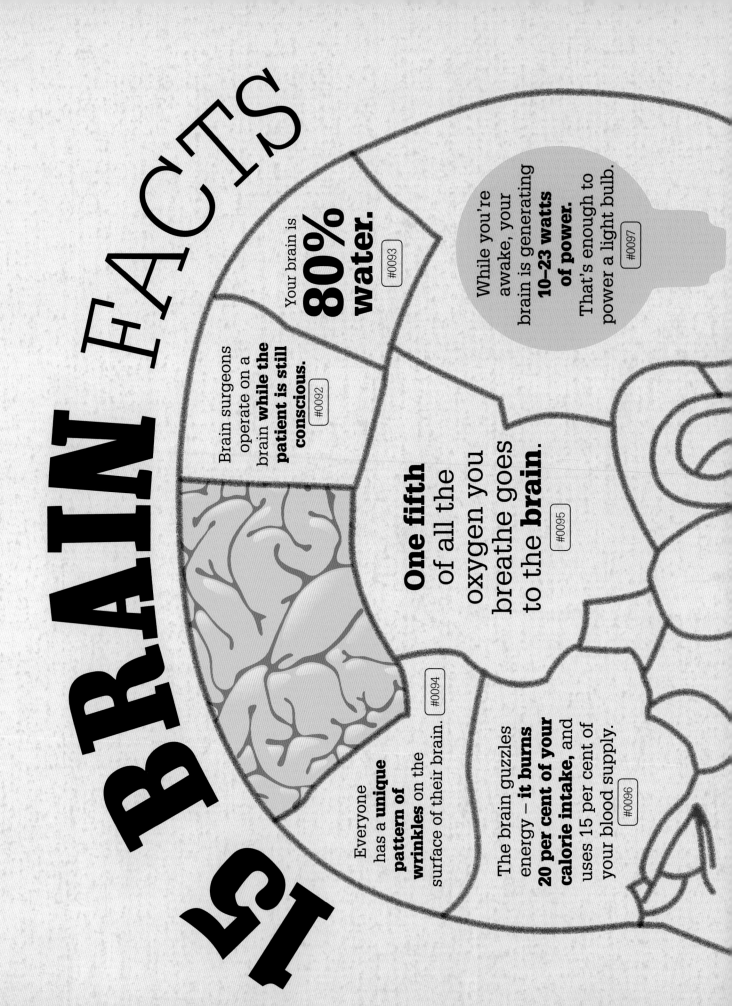

Brain surgeons operate on a brain **while the patient is still conscious.** #0092

Your brain is **80% water.** #0093

While you're awake, your brain is generating **10–23 watts of power.** That's enough to power a light bulb. #0097

**One fifth** of all the oxygen you breathe goes to the **brain.** #0095

Everyone has a **unique pattern of wrinkles** on the surface of their brain. #0094

The brain guzzles energy – **it burns 20 per cent of your calorie intake,** and uses 15 per cent of your blood supply. #0096

In ancient Rome, headaches were treated by hitting the patient over the head with **electric fish.**

#0100

The tissue of the brain is the consistency of soft jelly.

#0105

In 2007, a 44-year-old Frenchman was found to have a hollow brain. He had lived a totally normal life.

#0101

**The brain keeps growing until you're about 20, and your personality keeps developing as it grows.**

#0104

Damage to the brain can change your personality, making you kinder or nastier.

#0106

Doctors sometimes send pulses of electricity through patients' brains. This is called electroconvulsive therapy. Doctors sometimes treat their mentally ill patients with

#0099

Your brain is highly active when you are asleep. It is busy giving you dreams and nightmares.

#0098

It is possible to grow human brain cells in a laboratory dish.

#0103

Special scans called MRI scans track the flow of blood through a live brain, showing which bits are active.

#0102

# 13 Skin and dandruff facts

The skin covering your body is your heaviest organ. Its three layers weigh a hefty **5 kilograms.** #0108

A wart is a **KNOBBLY CLUMP** of skin cells that grows when a virus gets into the skin. #0107

People with **Naegeli syndrome** don't have any fingerprints. #0109

If an average person stretched out all their skin, it would be about 2 m² – **the size of a large bed.** #0110

You shed just under **4 kg of skin each year –** that's about the weight of 40 apples. #0112

# Your dead SKIN CELLS

fall off you at a rate of **40,000 a minute.** #0113

One person will shed enough skin in a lifetime to fill a suitcase. #0114

If you collected all the skin shed in one day by the whole world, it would fill a four-storey house. #0115

Four out of five teenagers get **acne** – a condition that makes red bumps on your skin. #0111

# Dandruff

occurs when skin oil glues your dead skin cells into clumps that get trapped by hairs. #0117

Tar has been used to treat dandruff for hundreds of years. #0118

**Dandruff can be caused by a fungus in your hair.** #0119

If your skin is rubbed for too long, it makes a little fluid-filled cushion called a blister to protect itself. Beneath the fluid, the skin is safe from friction. #0116

31

# 14 HAIRY facts

Up to **100 hairs** fall out of your head every day. #0120

...covered... palms of your ...the soles of yo... and your lips...

...often used to mop up oil spills. #0123

The average head of human hair is strong enough to hold the weight of two adult elephants. #0122

...of bald people is ...phobia. #0124

A human has the same number of hairs on his or her body as a chimpanzee. #0125

Hair is made from keratin – the same stuff as your fingernails. #0126

The only part of your hair that isn't dead is the bit inside your skin. #0127

32

TRICHOTILLOMANIA is the urge to pull out... ...something...

...used to dye ...ce. #0129

In the 18th century, rich ...used to wear WIGS ...made from the hair of poor people. #0130

In ancient Rome, pigeon dung was used to dye hair **BLONDE.** #0131

The longest beard was grown by Hans Langseth. It was more than 5.5 m long – that's the height of three tall men standing on top of each other. #0132

**Only 1% of the world's population have red hair.** In the Middle Ages, redheads were often thought to be witches, werewolves or vampires! #0133

# 8 icky facts about babies

A baby's head is three quarters of the size it will be when the child becomes an adult, and a quarter of its total body weight. #0134

Inside the womb, a baby **turns somersaults,** and scratches itself with its fingernails. #0135

Babies are sometimes born with hair all over their heads, back, shoulders and face, especially if they are born early. #0136

A newborn baby **POOS** out its own body weight every 60 hours. #0137

Newborn babies have **green poo.** The colour is caused by digestive juices that have built up while the baby was in the womb. #0138

A baby will go through nearly
# 3000 nappies
a year. #0139

A newborn baby **wees** every 20 minutes. #0140

One in every
**2000**
babies is born
**with teeth.**
#0141

# ABOMINABLE
# ANIMALS

Penguins **vomit** food back into their mouths to **feed** **their chicks.**

#0142

# 8 FARM animal FACTS

A sheep's upper lip is **split in half.** The sheep can move each half separately to choose the best **plant leaves** to eat.

#0143

Male goats **PEE on themselves** to attract females.

#0144

**PIGS CAN'T SWEAT,** so they **roll around in mud** to stay cool.

#0145

A cow's four-chambered stomach releases lots of gas, making it a

# CHAMPION FARTER.

#0146

A gas called methane, found in **cow manure,** can be used to create **electricity.**

#0147

Cows often **stick their tongues up their own noses** to eat the salt and keep flies away.

#0148

**Humanure** is sewage that has been recycled to make **farm fertilizer.**

#0149

Newborn foals **eat their mother's poo.** This gives them useful stomach bacteria which help **digest food.**

#0150

39

# 2 DETESTABLE DOG FACTS

Dogs' noses are about **100,000 times better than humans'.** Some dogs can **smell dead bodies under water** or detect lung cancer by sniffing a person's breath.

#0151

The wetness around a dog's nose is **mucus,** which traps molecules for the dog to sniff. #0152

# 5 CRAZY CAT FACTS

A cat flea can jump **200 times** its own body length. #0153

Cats **swallow fur** while licking themselves clean, then **vomit it up** as hair-balls. #0154

Cats sometimes eat grass to make themselves sick. #0156

**Cats mark their territory by pooing around the garden, and even in the house.** #0155

Cats kill their prey with a **bite to the neck** that stops the prey from breathing. #0157

# 13 facts about vicious HUNTERS

**Ghost slugs suck up worms like spaghetti.** #0158

Wolverines can take down prey more than **five times bigger** than themselves, killing them with a powerful bite. #0159

To knock insects off low-hanging leaves, the archerfish shoots them with a **well-aimed jet of spit,** then swims over to pick up its meal. #0160

## THE PRAYING MANTIS
stabs prey, such as caterpillars, with its spiky legs before eating it. #0161

The Humboldt squid uses suckers on its tentacles to catch fish, then it tears them apart with its beak. #0162

A hyena's bite is so strong that it can crunch through bones. #0163

The tentacled water snake makes a splash with the tip of its tail so that frightened fish will swim away, straight into its mouth. #0164

**Ants slice up their prey using their mandibles (jaws) like**

## SCISSORS. #0165

A dog whelk feeds off a mussel by drilling a hole in its shell, and eating the soft body inside. #0166

The **Amazonian giant centipede** lurks on cave ceilings, and uses **VENOMOUS CLAWS** to stab passing bats, paralysing them.

#0167

Cheetahs can reach speeds of up to **100** km/h when they are chasing their prey.

#0168

A starfish digests its shellfish prey alive by pushing its stomach out through its mouth and inserting it into an opening in the victim's shell. #0169

Komodo dragon lizards have a **venomous bite.** The venom is produced by special glands in the lizard's mouth. #0170

# 10 MAN-EATER facts

Crocodiles often have their mouths open, but it's not because they're hungry, it's because they **sweat through their mouths**. #0171

A Nile crocodile called **GUSTAVE** is thought to have killed **300 PEOPLE.** #0172

Crocodiles and alligators spin their prey around in a 'death roll' to kill it. #0173

Wolves have been known to tear at people's throats with their teeth. #0174

*Sharks do bite humans, but it is usually by mistake.* #0175

**Tigers** almost always **attack their prey from behind...** #0176

*...So, in India, workers wear masks on the backs of their heads to keep hungry tigers away.* #0177

The man-eating Leopard of Rudraprayag killed **more than 125 people** before it was shot in 1926. #0178

Human remains were found in the stomach of a brown bear called Kesagake, who terrorized a Japanese village in 1915. #0179

**If you come across a bear, DO NOT turn your back or run away. The bear may see this as weakness, and ATTACK.** #0180

# 11 FACTS ABOUT DEFENCE TACTICS

**A deep-sea shrimp** escapes danger by shooting out streams of **bioluminescent** glue in the dark, confusing the predator with **blobs** of **light.**

#0181

**The sea cucumber shoots its sticky guts at predators.**

#0182

An **octopus** sends out **clouds** of **dark ink** to confuse predators.

#0183

**Sperm whales** blast **poo** into the water as a defence, stirring it up into a brown cloud.

#0184

Some starfish **lose limbs** and **regrow** them. A whole **new starfish** can grow from just **one arm.**

#0185

Opossums **pretend to be DEAD** if in danger. They lie still for up to four hours, making a vile smell and **leaking green fluid from their bottoms.**
#0186

If a turkey vulture is attacked, it **vomits chunks of meat and sick** at the face of its attacker. #0187

The skunk uses its **bottom muscles** to shoot out its **stinky** spray over **6 m.** #0188

The Iberian ribbed newt can **push its razor sharp ribs outwards.** It coats them in runny poison as a double defence. #0189

Some horned lizards **spout blood** from their **eyes.** The spray can travel up to **30 cm.** #0190

Lots of lizards drop off their tails to confuse attackers. The tail will keep **wriggling** for up to 10 minutes to **distract the enemy** while the lizard escapes. #0191

47

# 9 POISON AND VENOM facts

The land snake with the **most lethal** venom is the **Australian inland taipan.**
#0192

The **most potent snake venom** of all comes from a Pacific sea snake, but it is peaceful, and won't attack unless very scared.
#0193

In India, **46,000** people die from snake bites a year – that's more than anywhere else in the world.
#0194

Some snake venoms work by shutting down the victim's body so that it is still alive but cannot move.
#0195

The **deadly puffer fish** is a delicacy in Japan, and chefs have to take great care to remove the poison. Even so, about 12 people die each year from eating this fish. #0196

The **golden poison frog** has enough deadly poison in it to kill **10 to 20** people. #0197

There are millions of poisonous cane toads in Australia. Dogs sometimes die after licking their toxic skin. #0198

The male **platypus** has venomous spurs on its heels. It uses these to fight other males during the mating season. #0199

Stonefish have.....
**13 venom-filled spines.** #0200

# 4 FACTS ABOUT
# CUCKOO BABIES

Cuckoos lay **their eggs** in **other birds'** nests… #0201

… The cuckoo egg **hatches first,** and **throws** any other **eggs** or **chicks** out of the nest… #0202

… The 'parents' do **not realize what has happened,** and feed the baby cuckoo as if it were their own… #0203

… If the other bird realizes and gets rid of the cuckoo egg, **the adult cuckoo will come back and destroy the whole nest.** #0204

# 5 ANIMAL CANNIBAL FACTS

When tadpoles hatch, they will eat any eggs they find nearby, as well as smaller tadpoles.
#0205

Baby caecilians feed by **gnawing off bits of their mother's skin.**
#0206

Adult polar bears, chimps, pigs, hamsters and wolf spiders have been known to

## EAT THEIR OWN BABIES.
#0207

Spider babies of the species Stegodyphus lineatus **gobble up their own mother** as their first meal.
#0208

The first grey nurse shark babies to hatch from their eggs will **eat their brothers and sisters.**
#0209

51

# 12 FACTS ABOUT PESKY Parasites

The **average human** body carries between **1 and 2.5 kg** of parasitic bacteria (organisms that feed on a larger host).

#0210

## The largest parasitic worm ever found

was **8.5 m** long. It was found living in a female sperm whale's womb.

#0211

A tapeworm **can live inside a human gut** for up to 20 years.

#0212

Tiny **white pinworms** live in your gut, but move to your

# BOTTOM

to lay eggs.

#0213

**Parasitic worm eggs** get into soil through animal droppings... #0214

... There can be **THOUSANDS** of parasitic worm eggs **in one handful of soil**. #0215

Flukes are parasitic worms found in **FISH, CATTLE AND SHEEP.** Humans can also become infected by swimming in fluke-infested water. #0217

Hookworms can live in your intestine, sucking on **YOUR BLOOD.** #0216

Humans can become infected with the parasite *Toxoplasma gondii* by eating undercooked meat, or coming into contact with **infected cat poo**. #0218

Thorny-headed worms hatch inside pond crustaceans, which are then eaten by ducks. The worm reproduces inside the duck, and its **eggs come out in the duck's poo.** They are then eaten by a crustacean, and the cycle begins again. #0219

**A female flea** sucks up to **15 TIMES** **her own body weight in blood every day.**

#0220

The **tongue-eating** louse **EATS THE TONGUE** of its fish victim, and lives in its place. #0221

# 9 FACTS ABOUT
# WEIRD LOOKING ANIMALS

The deep-sea angler lures prey towards its huge mouth using a glowing light at the end of a strange 'fishing rod' attached to its head. #0222

## WHEN PLAICE ARE BORN...

... they are shaped like ordinary fish. As they grow, one eye moves round and over the fish's head to be on the same side as the other one. #0223

## DUMBO OCTOPUSES

have floppy fins that look like big ears. #0224

• The nose of the proboscis monkey can stretch out more than 10 cm. #0225

**The hagfish** produces slime to help it wriggle free from captors. #0226

The naked mole rat is hairless and wrinkled, but it is a tough critter that never gets cancer. #0227

**THE BLOBFISH** is a gloopy blob of jelly with almost no muscle. #0228

The 22 fleshy snouts on a **star-nosed mole** have more than 25,000 touch sensors to help it feel its way underground. #0229

**Marabou storks** poke their heads into dead bodies to eat. Their heads are bald so they don't get any blood on their feathers. #0230

# 10 SPIDER FACTS

The female black widow often eats the male after mating.
#0231

Poisonous black widows have been found **hiding in bunches of grapes**.
#0232

To invade high ground, small spiders can release several threads, which form a **PARACHUTE**. Spiders have been seen as high up as 3000 m.
#0234

The venomous redback spider of Australia has been known to **lurk beneath toilet seats**.
#0233

**Ogre-faced spiders** weave a web between their front legs. They use the web like a net to catch any prey that flies into it.
#0235

The **biggest spider in the world** is the Goliath bird-eating spider, which is as big as a dinner plate.

#0236

**Spitting spiders** spit a mixture of venom and glue at a victim. This sticks the prey in one place and kills it. #0237

Venomous **Brazilian wandering spiders** can grow up to 13 cm wide, and have been found hidden in bunches of bananas.

#0238

The venom of the brown recluse spider is necrotic, meaning that it **rots your flesh**. #0239

Spiders can't digest anything solid. They dissolve food by **injecting digestive juices into their prey**, then they suck up the gloop left behind.

#0240

# 11 facts about WORMS

Lugworms eat **sand,** while earthworms eat **soil.** #0241

A worm is covered in **slimy mucus,** which helps it to **absorb oxygen through its skin.** #0242

Earthworms lay their eggs wrapped in a protective cocoon made of **SLIMY MUCUS**. #0243

Earthworms and lugworms **poo wiggly tubes** called worm casts. #0244

**Earthworm poo** is a great fertilizer for the soil. #0245

The **thousands of tiny hairs** on an earthworm help it to grip the soil. #0246

If a worm stays out in the sun for too long, **IT DRIES OUT** and dies. #0247

## EARTHWORM BODIES

are made up of segments. If a worm loses its back end, it can grow a new one as long as there are enough segments left at the front… #0248

… **The new back end of an earthworm grows back a lighter colour.** #0249

The largest worms live in hot countries, and grow up to **3M long.** #0250

**An earthworm is a hermaphrodite, which means it is both male and female.** #0251

59

# 6 **Slithery** snail **Facts**

Snails move by **squeezing** and **relaxing** their muscles bit by bit, so they make a **rippling** motion. #0252

The giant **AFRICAN snail grows** up to **30 cm** long and lays an egg **6 cm** wide. #0253

As they move, snails create a trail of mucus. The **mucus lubricates the ground,** allowing snails to move more easily. #0254

Boiled snail pulp was once used to treat burns, and **SNAIL MUCUS** was **smeared on sore skin.** #0255

Some fish **EAT** water snails by **sucking them out of their shells.** #0256

**Garden snails** have over **14,000 teeth** on their radula (tongue). #0257

# 4 **Slimy slug** Facts

Most slugs eat **plants,** but **some will hunt down** other slugs by following their **sticky trail.**

#0258

## SLUG GOO

has tiny fibres in it that help the slug to climb up walls.

#0260

A slug's bum is on the back of its head. #0259

Slugs produce a constant trail of **GOO** to stop them from **drying out** and dying. #0261

# 8 CREEPY COCKROACH facts

Ancient Greeks used to **grind up cockroaches** into a paste to treat wounds.

#0262

Giant rhino cockroaches are kept as pets by some people. They grow up to

# 8 cm

long, and like to be stroked.

#0263

Cockroaches leave brown **POO** marks wherever they go. #0264

Cockroaches sometimes drink moisture from the
# MOUSTACHES
of sleeping men. #0265

The **tiny hairs** on a cockroach **pick up germs** as they move through drains. #0266

**A cockroach can survive for up to a month after losing its head.** #0267

A cockroach
**sheds its skin** between
**10 and 12 times**
during its lifetime. #0268

When disturbed, the Florida woods cockroach lets off a foul smell, so it is also known as the
## STINKING COCKROACH.
#0269

# 6 FACTS ABOUT DEEP-SEA MONSTERS

The **Sloane's viperfish's** teeth are so large that it has to make its jaws vertical to be able to open its mouth wide enough to swallow its prey. #0270

The **giant squid** has a hard beak, shaped like a parrot's. Scientists believe the squid uses it to dismember or paralyse its prey. #0271

**Gulper eels** are almost all mouth and no body – they have giant hinged mouths, and can eat animals much larger than themselves. #0272

**Flashlight fish** have luminous bacteria behind their retinas, giving them glowing eyes, which they can blink on to attract prey, or off to avoid predators. #0274

The **goblin shark** looks for food with its snout. It catches prey with a jaw that can reach right out of its mouth. #0273

**Zombie worms** dissolve holes in whale bones, then live inside the bones. #0275

65

# 10 FACTS ABOUT
# BUGS in the home

The **house centipede kills prey** by **injecting venom** with its fangs.
#0276

A daddy-long-legs spider **catches its prey by weaving a cocoon**, rendering its victim helpless.
#0277

**Bed bugs** are flat, button-shaped parasites that **live in mattresses** and **drink your blood** at night.
#0278

Carpet beetle larvae are also known as **WOOLLY BEARS** because they **love to eat natural fibres** found in items such as carpets, curtains and clothes.
#0279

The **colossus earwig** grows up to **6 cm long.**
#0280

Earwigs come out at night, eating other insects, eggs and even each other.
#0281

You shed enough flakes of skin in one day to feed **one million dust mites.**
#0282

Between two and **three million dust mites live in the average bed** mattress.
#0283

Dust mites only live for a couple of months... #0284

... But during that time they produce up to

**200** **times their own body weight in POO.** #0285

# HIDEOUS HISTORY

The Vikings believed that the first people came from the **sweat** of a **mythical creature**, the **earth** from his **flesh**, the **hills** from his **bones** and the **oceans** from his **blood.** #0286

# 6 STONE AGE LIFE facts

## In 1950, Tollund Man, a 2500-year-old corpse, was found **naturally mummified in a peat bog.**

#0288

Cave paintings were made **30,000** years ago using paint made from dirt or charcoal mixed with spit, animal fat or urine. #0287

Ancient human skulls from

# 160,000 years ago

have been found with cut marks in them, suggesting **CANNIBALISM**.

#0289

Stone Age people stitched up wounds using **needles made of bone,** and **thread made of muscle tissue.** #0290

In 1991, the **5000-year-old** body of a hunter nicknamed Ötzi was found **perfectly preserved in ice** in the Alps, Europe. #0291

During the last

ICE AGE

people built houses using **mammoth bones** as struts. #0292

71

# 12 ANCIENT ROMAN FACTS

Roman fortune tellers would **predict the future** by studying the guts of **sacrificed animals.**
#0293

It was considered polite **to belch** in ancient Rome.
#0297

## PUBLIC TOILETS

were a **line of holes** in a long stone seat with running water below to flush the waste away. #0294

Romans cleaned their clothes **with pee.**
#0298

Men would go to public toilets to be social and **have a chat.** #0295

Romans wiped their bums with **a sponge on a stick.** #0296

**People visited the Colosseum in Rome to watch gladiators fight. Sometimes the crowds called for the loser to be killed.** #0299

After a death in the arena, a referee would hit the corpse over the head with a mallet, to show that it now belonged to Pluto, god of the underworld. #0300

In lunch intervals at the Colosseum, criminals were thrown into a no-win fight with **hungry lions and tigers.** #0301

**Drinking gladiator BLOOD was recommended by Roman doctors to treat epilepsy.** #0302

**Ostrich brains** were a delicacy in ancient Rome. #0303

Roman fathers were shown their newborn babies and could decide whether they lived or died. #0304

# 17 facts about AZTECS

Aztec Emperor Tlacaelel started a **war** so that he could **gather more prisoners to sacrifice** to the gods. #0305

Only wealthy Aztecs were allowed to wear feathers. #0306

The Aztecs used **cocoa beans** as money. #0307

Priests would cut themselves... #0308 ...spill the blood onto paper... #0309 ...and burn it as an offering to the gods. #0310

When someone died, the Aztecs might kill a dog and bury it with the person, **so that it could guide them on their journey through the afterlife.** #0311

It was not uncommon for someone who was poor to **sell their own children into slavery**... #0312

...Many Aztecs would also sell *themselves* into slavery... #0313

...Some remained slaves most of their lives. #0314

Doctors in ancient Mexico treated earache by pouring **hot liquid rubber** into the ear. #0317

Poor Aztecs would eat a scum made of algae, known as **'stone dung'**. #0318

An annual ritual to the

# RAIN GOD,

Tlaloc, involved making a child cry. #0319

**Smallpox killed 3 million** Aztecs when the Spanish brought the disease to Mexico. #0320

Aztecs played a ball game called **Ulamaliztli**. The ball was said to represent the head of a **sacrificed victim**. #0315

The losing team would then be **sacrificed**. #0316

Ruler Moctezuma II was **killed by his own people** for surrendering to the Spaniards. #0321

75

## 9 facts about
# EGYPTIAN MUMMIES

It took 70 days for the ancient Egyptians to make a mummy out of a dead body. #0322

First, they cut open the body with a **sharp stone,** then removed the **stomach, lungs and other organs,** and put them in jars near the body. #0323

The **HEART was left inside the body.** It was thought to be vital for the **AFTERLIFE.** #0324

A sacred **scarab beetle** was placed on the heart. #0325

Using a hammer and chisel, they knocked a **hole** into the nose bone and hooked out the **brain**. #0326

**The Egyptians thought the brain was unimportant, and threw it away.** #0327

Then they stuffed the body with **bandages** and **sawdust,** covered it completely with salt and left it for a month to dry out. #0328

**After the month, they wrapped the mummy in RESIN-SOAKED BANDAGES while casting spells over it.** #0329

Pharaoh Tutankhamun's mummy shows that he may have **died from gangrene** (a stinking flesh-rotting infection) after he broke his leg. #0330

77

# 11 Facts about CASTLES

Medieval soldiers attacking a castle would hurl

## DEAD ANIMALS

and **human heads** at it from giant wooden catapults... #0331

...The rotting corpses would **spread disease** inside the castle. #0332

Lords would **cut off a criminal's head, and stick it on a pole** above the castle's portcullis (entrance) as a warning to others. #0333

## CATS AND DOGS

were kept to **kill the rats** that would eat the castle's food supply. #0334

Castle guests would leave their coats in the **'garderobe'**, which was **inside the castle toilet.** They thought the pong protected the clothes from fleas. #0335

Castle floors were covered in straw. Mixed in with the straw could be **grease, bones, spit and even dog poo.** #0336

**Murder-holes** were put in the ceilings of a passageway so defenders could **pour burning oil** onto attackers. #0338

Workers called **gong farmers** had to clean up the mess. #0339

**Prisoners were often thrown into deep holes** called

## *oubliettes.*

The name means 'forgotten place' in French, and prisoners were often left there to die. #0340

In 1203, Phillip II's soldiers surrounded Château Gaillard in Normandy, France. They broke into the castle by **crawling through a sewage trench**. #0341

# 11 Perilous Pirate facts

The worst pirates were **hanged,** and their bodies were **covered in tar** and left to **rot publicly** in an iron cage. #0342

After **William Kidd** was caught in 1701, his corpse was left to rot for **three years.** #0343

Pirates would collect fresh food when they landed, but on ship it quickly went **stale or mouldy.** Not eating enough good food often made pirates sick – their **teeth fell out** and their **skin went pale**. #0344

**Henry Morgan** accidentally blew up his own ship, killing 350 men. #0345

Edward Teach was also known as **Blackbeard**. When he attacked a ship, he'd tie lit **gunpowder** fuses into his beard to scare his victims. #0346

Edward Teach liked to drink **rum** mixed with **gunpowder**. #0347

Pirate flags were designed to **terrify people**, sending the message **'surrender quickly or die'**. #0348

## MINOR OFFENCES
**were punished by flogging pirates with a knotted rope.** #0349

**As punishment,** a pirate might be dragged on a rope under the ship... #0350

**... He would either drown** or be slashed by the razor-sharp barnacles on the ship's hull. #0351

A cheating fellow pirate would be left on a desert island with little food or water, and a **loaded pistol** to kill himself #0352

# 12 facts about Crazy Royals

**English King** Henry II had a jester called Roland the Farter, who would **fart on demand.** #0354

English King Henry VIII had a groom of the stool – a man who **wiped his bottom** for him. #0353

To keep guests entertained at a feast, Roman Emperor Caligula would **behead** criminals in between courses. #0355

When his sister died, Caligula was so upset **he banned people from laughing, on pain of DEATH**. He also banned them from taking a bath. #0356

**Louis XIV** of France only took **three baths** in his lifetime. #0357

In 1762, Korean Prince Sado was **locked in a rice chest** by his father. He died after eight days. #0358

King Nabonidus of Babylon thought he was a **goat,** and insisted on **grazing in a field.** #0359

Duke Gian Gastone of Tuscany, Italy, **stayed in a stinking bed for 7 years,** refusing to get up. #0360

Don Carlos, son of Spanish King Phillip II, forced a shoemaker to **eat a pair of shoes** that weren't up to standard. #0362

By the time he died, aged 55, Henry VIII was **covered in boils** and so **overweight** that he couldn't move about by himself. #0361

Anna of Russia built an **ICE PALACE** to celebrate the marriage of a prince she did not like. She made the married couple stay there on their wedding night. #0363

When they had finished building St Basil's Cathedral in Moscow, Russian Tsar Ivan the Terrible had the designers **blinded,** so they could never build anything better. #0364

# 7 Bad medicine facts

In ancient Egypt, rubbing your eyes with **mashed tortoise brains** was a treatment for bad eyesight. #0365

Egyptian doctors recommended **treating toothache** by holding a **freshly killed mouse** on your gums. #0366

For centuries, Europeans thought the world was made of four kinds of things, called **'humours',** which were represented in the body by:

yellow bile

blood

black bile

phlegm

#0367

In the Middle Ages, doctors treated many illnesses with **bloodletting** – taking some of the patient's blood. It usually just made the patient **even weaker.** #0368

An ancient surgery called **trepanning** involved **drilling a hole** in the patient's skull. #0369

One attempted **cure for the plague** involved strapping a **plucked chicken to your body.** #0370

To make **rotten teeth fall out,** Tudor dentists used a mixture of **poo and honey.** #0371

85

# 9 Freaky facts about Fashion

In Europe in the 1100s, shoes with **very long, curly toes** were fashionable. They were called **'pikases'** because they had a pointed end, like a pike.
#0372

Before the 19th century, there was no such thing as a fashion model. Instead, designers used **little dolls** to show their fashions to customers.
#0373

In the 1600s, fashionable men and women wore **white make-up** made of **LEAD**. The lead was poisonous, and rotted their skin.
#0374

In the 17th century, Louis XIII of France wanted to hide his baldness so he began a fashion for the periwig, a lavish wig for men. **A bigger wig made the wearer more fashionable.**
#0375

In 17th century France, the bleach used to colour clothes was made from **URINE**. #0376

French leader Napoleon Bonaparte first added buttons to jacket sleeves. He wanted to stop soldiers **wiping their runny noses** on their sleeves. #0377

Aristocrats in Tibet wore sleeves so long that their hands were hidden. It showed that they were **too posh** to do manual work. #0378

In the 1880s, many women wore **bustles** under their dresses. These were frames or pads designed to **make their bottoms look huge.** #0379

Many Chinese women were **crippled by the fashion for tiny feet.** Young girls' toes were **broken** and wrapped tightly in bandages to stop their feet from growing. #0380

87

# 7 CHILDREN AT WORK FACTS

Young crossing sweepers would clear the streets of **rubbish** and **horse poo** so that rich people wouldn't get their clothes dirty. #0381

In ancient Sparta, **7-year-old boys** were sent to **military school.** They were made to sleep on beds made of sharp reeds, whipped, and trained to fight using animals and slaves. #0382

Kids in the 1800s collected **dog and cat poo.** The poo was used to soften leather before it could be made into clothes and bags. #0383

**In coal mines,** trucks full of coal were pushed along narrow tunnels by children. #0384

In 19th-century Europe, matches were made by girls using **poisonous phosphorus.** #0385

Some children in mines would stay underground up to **18 hours** a day. #0386

Because they were **small enough** to fit up chimneys, Victorian children were sent up flues to **sweep them out.** #0387

# 7 FACTS ABOUT FILTHY FACTORIES

Men who live near the weapons factory in Dzerzinsk, Russia, **die at an average age of 42** due to the water pollution.

#0388

A chemical factory in Ranipet, India, has made a pile of toxic waste that weighs **1.5 million tonnes.**

#0389

**Slag heaps** are large mounds of waste that are piled up around mining towns. In the past these heaps have **collapsed,** creating dangerous landslides.

#0390

90

A spill from a pesticide factory in Bhopal, India, created a toxic cloud that killed up to 20,000 people.

#0391

When car-manufacturer Henry Ford visited a slaughterhouse, he saw the dead cows hanging in a line, and how quickly they were processed. After this visit, he came up with the idea of using an 'assembly line' in his factories.

#0392

Luddites were people who protested against the rise of factories by **smashing machines** and attacking merchants.

#0393

Women working in British arms factories during World War I were nicknamed **'canaries'** because their skin was stained yellow by the sulphur used to make weapons.

#0394

91

# 10 DREADFUL DESPOTS FACTS

Turkish Sultan Abdul Hamid II was so **scared of intruders** that he paid someone to sleep with **loaded pistols** and booby-trapped the staircase with **tripwires** and **guns**. #0395

In 1893, American James Harden-Hickey claimed an Atlantic island, declared himself king **James I**, and printed his **own money.** #0397

Maximilien Robespierre was a leader of the **French Revolution.** He sent his enemies to the **guillotine,** but in the end was guillotined himself. #0396

## Ivan the Terrible,
the 16th-century Russian Tsar, once dressed an archbishop in **bear furs** and then had him hunted to death by a pack of **ferocious dogs.** #0398

Turkmenistan's dictator Saparmurat Niyazov banned **ballet, opera** and the **circus** in 2001, and forbade men to **have beards** or **long hair** in 2004. #0399

92

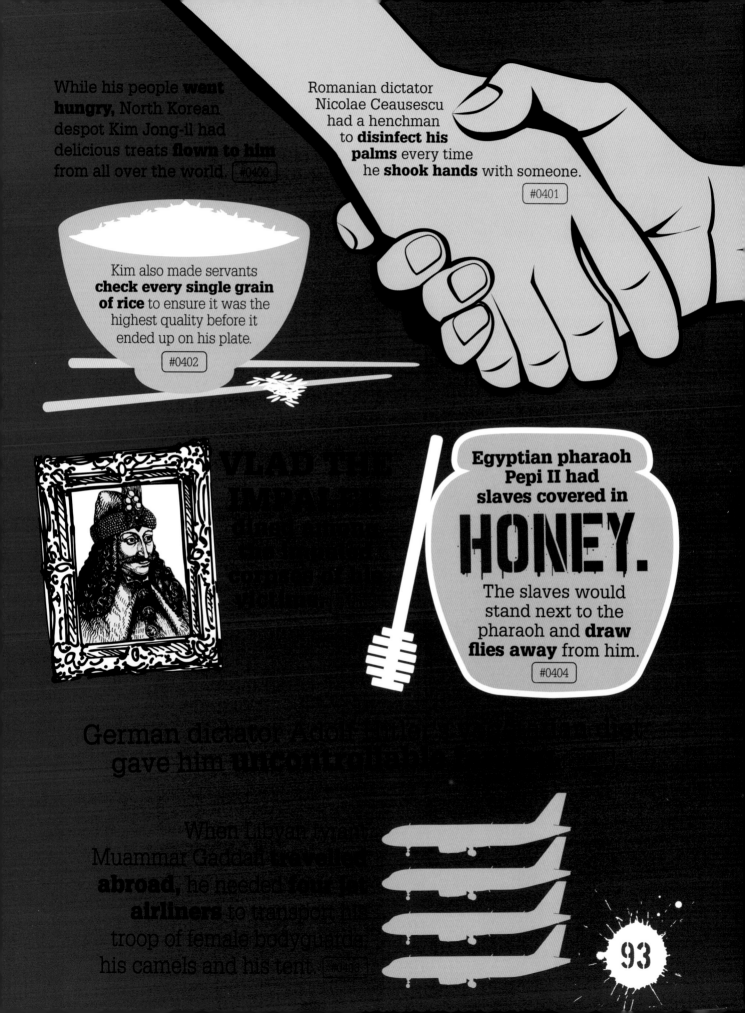

While his people **went hungry,** North Korean despot Kim Jong-il had delicious treats **flown to him** from all over the world. #0400

Romanian dictator Nicolae Ceausescu had a henchman to **disinfect his palms** every time he **shook hands** with someone. #0401

Kim also made servants **check every single grain of rice** to ensure it was the highest quality before it ended up on his plate. #0402

VLAD THE IMPALER

Egyptian pharaoh Pepi II had slaves covered in

# HONEY.

The slaves would stand next to the pharaoh and **draw flies away** from him. #0404

German dictator Adolf Hitler gave him uncontrollable

When Libyan tyrant Muammar Gaddafi travelled abroad, he needed four jet airliners to transport his troop of female bodyguards, his camels and his tent.

# 10 FACTS ABOUT
# INTREPID
## EXPLORERS

Polar explorers used to **eat their sled dogs** during the course of an expedition.

#0407

British explorer Ranulph Fiennes **sawed off his own fingers** that had been damaged by frostbite.

#0408

Some of the **health effects** of long polar trips include **SICKNESS, DIZZINESS, HAIR AND NAIL LOSS AND EYES AND SKIN GOING YELLOW.**

#0409

Swiss Antarctic explorer Xavier Mertz died after eating too much **dog liver.** He was poisoned by the high level of vitamin A.

#0410

In 1819, British explorer John Franklin led an expedition in which 11 of the 20 explorers died. In 1845, he led an expedition to the Arctic, and the **whole crew died.**

#0411

Italian desert marathon runner Mauro Prosperi **survived for 10 days** after getting lost in a windstorm by drinking the **blood of two bats.**

#0412

British explorer John Hanning Speke **survived dangerous expeditions** around Africa, **but died** after accidentally **shooting himself** while at home in England.

#0413

Vietnamese fisherman Bui Duc Phuc survived for **14 days** after a strong current swept him out to sea by **drinking his own pee.**

#0414

While climbing in the Andes in 1985, British climber Joe Simpson fell **50 m** and broke his leg. It took him four days to struggle to safety.

#0415

When a huge boulder fell on explorer **Aron Ralston** in Utah, USA in 2003, he had to **cut off his trapped hand with a penknife** to escape.

#0416

95

# 11 facts about Crazy Artists

After a fight with fellow artist Gauguin, Vincent van Gogh **cut off his own ear.** #0417

The poet Tennyson liked to do an impression of a man sitting on the loo. #0418

The poet Swinburne once slid down the banister naked at a dinner party. #0419

Romantic poet Lord Byron lived with a variety of pets, including a crocodile, a goat and a heron. #0420

Surrealist artist Marcel Duchamp made a piece called *Fountain*, which was nothing more than a urinal. #0421

Writer Oscar Wilde kept a **dead lobster** that he would take for walks.
#0422

Performance artist Chris Burden once nailed himself to a car.
#0423

A Belgian artist made a sculpture using **8000 slices of ham.** As the meat began to stink, it attracted swarms of flies, turning it into 'living sculpture'. #0424

The artist Salvador Dalí was afraid of grasshoppers – when they appear in his work, they are used as a symbol of destruction, waste and fear.
#0425

**Artist Damien Hirst pickled a large tiger shark in formaldehyde, and put it on show in a tank.** #0427

97

# 4 SCARY SCIENCE

Scientists believe they might be able to restore the sight of blind people by studying the **eyes** of insects. They believe they can copy the compound eyes to replicate 'INSECT-VISION'.

#0428

# 11 MAD SCIENTIST facts

Dutch scientist Antoni van Leeuwenhoek **discovered bacteria** by studying the **plaque on his own teeth** under a microscope.

#0429

Inventor Leonardo da Vinci cut up **dead horses and humans** to learn how their bodies worked. #0430

In 1796, English scientist Edward Jenner **deliberately infected an 8-year-old** boy with a mild disease called **cowpox.** He found that the boy became immune to **deadly smallpox** and he was able to create a **vaccine** against the terrible disease that saved millions of lives. #0431

British physicist Sir Isaac Newton was believed to have had a **mental breakdown** in 1692. However, his strange behaviour is now thought to have been caused by **mercury poisoning.** #0432

In the 18th century, Johann Konrad Dippel invented an oil that he thought would help people to **live forever.** However, it was only useful as an animal repellent and a poison. #0433

In the 18th century, Italian scientist Luigi Galvani made a **dead frog's legs twitch** using

# electricity.

This made him think he could use electricity to bring the dead back to life. #0434

When Christian Schönbein mopped up acid with his wife's cotton apron, it caused the apron to explode. He had discovered nitrocellulose or **'guncotton'.** #0435

In the 18th century, US doctor Stubbins Ffirth tested how **yellow fever** might be spread by drinking

## INFECTED VOMIT.

His theories were wrong, however, because yellow fever is spread by mosquitoes. #0436

As well as helping develop the electrical supply you use today, Nikola Tesla also claimed to have invented a **'death ray' weapon,** an **earthquake machine** and a method for **splitting the world in two.** #0437

In the early 19th century, Andrew Ure, a Scottish doctor, tried to bring a **hanged man back to life by sending an electric current through his neck.** #0438

Ilya Ivanovich Ivanov tried to create a

## HUMANZEE

(a human-chimpanzee hybrid) in 1927. #0439

# 8 foul facts about INVENTIONS

In the early 1900s, scientist **Marie Curie** discovered the radioactive elements **polonium and radium,** but she fell sick after carrying tubes containing the **dangerous chemicals in her pockets.**

#0440

In 1867, William Bullock developed **gangrene** and died after crushing his foot in **his own invention** – the rotary printing press. #0441

The toilet snorkel was invented in 1982 to provide **clean air via the toilet bowl, in case of fire.** #0442

## In 1995, the babyvac

was invented to **clean snot out of babies' noses** so that they could breathe more easily. #0443

In 2005, scientists in Singapore created a battery powered by

# URINE.

#0444

In 1908, George Hogan designed an alarm clock that **tipped water onto a sleeping person** to wake them up.

#0445

The Aspire Assist Aspiration Therapy System was invented in 2013. It is a **weight-loss device** that pumps food out of your stomach before your body can digest it. #0446

Scientists in Japan have invented a **FART RECORDER** that **analyses a fart's smell** and then recreates it using a mixture of chemicals.

#0447

103

# 9 more vile INVENTIONS

In 2009, designer Mike Thomson invented a **lamp that needs a DROP OF BLOOD to make it work.** He hoped it would make people think twice before turning on the lamp!

#0448

In 2008, New York unveiled its first **automated pay toilet.** The user has a **15-minute time limit,** after which the door flies open.

#0449

The White Goat machine can recycle used office paper into toilet paper in about **30 minutes.** Unfortunately, the machine is the size of **two wardrobes.**

#0450

The Bird Trap and Cat Feeder was a fake birdhouse that lured birds in and then trapped them. Cats could then come along and eat the caged bird.

#0451

104

## Hair-in-a-Can

was meant to be spray-on hair to cover bald patches. It looked so bad that most people preferred being bald.

#0452

Thomas Midgley Jr's inventions have caused a lot of **damage to the environment.** As well as **leaded petrol,** he developed **CFCs**. These are the gases that were found in **fridges and aerosols** and created a huge hole in the **ozone layer.** #0453

American scientists are developing a **3D food** printer, which will allow you to 'print off' edible food, using raw food as **'ink'.**

#0454

## SMELL-O-VISION

was an invention to **release scent** during a movie. It was used briefly in the 1960s but was so unpopular that it has **not been attempted since.** #0455

Moviemakers are working on a **'touch jacket'** that will make your skin crawl and send shivers up your spine while you watch a movie. #0456

# 11 FACTS ABOUT EXPERIMENTS

In 1928, while trying to perfect blood transfusion, Russian scientist Alexander Bogdanov fatally injected himself with infected blood.

#0457

In 1964, Australian doctor Jack Barnes allowed himself and his 9-year-old son to be **stung by a jellyfish** and proved that it was the cause of the dangerous **Irukandji syndrome.**

#0458

During World War II, the US tried attaching **bombs to bats.** However, some of the bats roosted under a fuel tanker and set fire to a US air base.

#0459

In 2004, scientists at the University of Washington, USA, received **poo through the post,** because park rangers in Africa sent them elephant dung to analyse the DNA. The scientists created a poo-inspired **map of the elephant population** across Africa.

#0460

During the Cold War, the CIA fitted a **spy cat** with hidden microphones. Unfortunately, a taxi crushed it on its first test run.

#0461

In 1997, American scientists **grew a human-shaped ear on the back of a mouse.** #0465

Giovanni Grassi ate **roundworm eggs** to prove how the parasites are transmitted. He found that the eggs **passed through his body** and hatched in his **own poo.** #0463

To find out how humans could live alone in space, French geologist Michel Siffre lived inside an **underground glacier** with no daylight for two months. #0464

In 1938, John Deering volunteered to be monitored **during his execution** so that doctors could learn what happened to the body during death by gun shot. #0467

In 1942, Professor Lawrence Leshant conducted a sleep-learning experiment on boys at a summer camp who were diagnosed as chronic nail-biters. Every night, while they slept, he played a repeat message: **'My fingernails taste terribly bitter.'** By the end of the summer, 40 per cent had kicked the habit. #0462

In 1901, Ivan Pavlov observed that dogs salivated when they were given food, so he rang a bell at the same time. Soon, he was able to make the dogs drool just by ringing the bell, even if there was **no food.** #0466

# 7 facts about STINKY SCIENCE

At the end of the 20th century, American chemists developed the **world's worst smell**, a foul mixture known as **STENCH SOUP**.

#0468

**Stench soup** is the **ultimate** non-lethal **stink weapon** – anyone who smells it will run away in the opposite direction.

#0469

**Hydrogen sulphide**, a common chemical compound, is both **dangerous** and **disgusting**. It is POISONOUS, FLAMMABLE, EXPLOSIVE – and it smells of **ROTTEN EGGS**.

#0470

# AMMONIA

can be found in FERTILIZERS, CLEANING PRODUCTS, HUMAN KIDNEYS and on ripe cheeses such as CAMEMBERT. Unfortunately, it smells like **URINE!** #0471

A SMELLY SUBSTANCE called **Standard Bathroom Malodor** is used to test deodorizers and air fresheners. It smells like **human poo**, only much stronger. #0472

**Farms are smelly** because the gases from the **animals' farts** and **poo** mix with dust particles in the air. #0473

A **dirty dishcloth** smells really **bad**, thanks to the millions of **YUCKY BACTERIA** growing on it. #0474

109

# 9 facts about CHEMICALS

**DDT (dichloro-diheyl-trichloreoethene)** was a popular insecticide, until it was found to poison birds and marine organisms, and affect human health. #0475

All of the **oxygen** you breathe on Earth is a plant waste product. #0476

In small doses, **nitroglycerin** can be used in heart medication. In large doses, it is used in explosives. #0477

**Sodium phosphate** can be used as a food additive – it is also used in soap. #0478

**Propylene glycol** is found in lime- or orange-flavoured foods and animal feed, but it is also found in antifreeze and **can be used to poison beetles.** #0479

While **fluoride** helps prevent tooth decay, **hydrofluoric acid** is so corrosive that it will dissolve glass. #0480

**Titanium dioxide,** used as food colouring in salad dressings, is also used in sunscreen and paint. #0481

Some lipsticks contain **lead**. This makes the lipstick mildly toxic – but only if it is eaten. #0482

**The hardest substance in your body is in your tooth enamel.** #0483

# 10 facts about BIOLOGY

The BROWN MARMORATED STINK BUG releases a **FOUL-SMELLING ODOUR** from holes in its abdomen.

#0484

On an average day, you will **inhale** about 1 l of other people's FART GASES.

#0485

The **Rafflesia arnoldii** is the largest flower on Earth. It attracts flies to pollinate it by producing a **stink** like **rotting meat**.

#0486

The **bird-dropping spider** has developed a **foolproof disguise** to avoid predators – it looks **exactly** like **bird poo!**

#0487

When you **blush**, your **stomach lining** turns **red**. #0488

There are more tiny organisms on the skin of one human than there are human beings on Earth. #0489

The **TURKEY VULTURE** scares off predators by VOMITING FOUL-SMELLING, SEMI-DIGESTED food. #0490

The turkey vulture also uses its own **poo** to cool its body. #0491

The **human body** contains enough **fat** to produce **seven bars of soap**. #0492

The tiny **GOLDEN DART FROG** is one of the most poisonous creatures in the world. Its skin is coated with **enough poison** to kill up to **20 HUMANS.** #0493

# 12 facts about SURGERY

**ANCIENT ROMANS**
practised plastic surgery to repair
**noses**, **eyes**, **lips** and **teeth**.
#0494

One procedure in **ancient Rome** was
the removal of **scar tissue** from the
back, because it implied that a man had
**turned his back in battle** and was a

# COWARD.
#0495

Most surgeries in
Renaissance times
**(14th–17th centuries)**
were performed in
**BARBER SHOPS.**
#0496

Many of the patients seen by
16th-century Italian surgeon
**GASPARE TAGLIACOZZI**
were treated for wounds caused by
**DUELS** or **STREET FIGHTS.**
#0497

Tagliacozzi created **new
noses** using **ARM TISSUE.**
However, the new nose could
fall off if the person
blew it too hard.
#0498

Australian artist Stelios Arcadious had an **EAR** grown from cells in a laboratory implanted in his arm to make him a living art exhibit. #0499

About **17 million** plastic surgery operations are carried out every year worldwide… #0500

…More take place in SWITZERLAND than any other country, with about **216 procedures** per **100,000 people** each year. #0501

In the Middle Ages, surgeons used **herbs** and **alcohol** as simple anaesthetics. #0502

The earliest form of surgery was **trepanning,** which involved cutting a small round hole in the head. #0503

In 2007, a man in Colorado, USA, had his **THUMBS NARROWED** so that he could **use his iPhone more efficiently.** #0504

Some fashion-conscious women have a **toe bone removed** so that they can wear slim-fitting shoes. #0505

# 14 facts about
# GENETICS

To save time on sheep shearing, Australian scientists developed a sheep whose **wool drops out** after it has reached a certain length.
#0506

In 1985, scientists developed **a pig** that grew so big it became crippled with arthritis.
#0507

Scientists have created a **POISONOUS CABBAGE.** Any hungry caterpillar that tries to eat it will **drop dead.** Luckily, the cabbage is harmless to humans!
#0508

To protect potato crops, scientists in the 1990s developed potato plants that would **die** if they became **infected by diseases or parasites.**
#0509

Phosphorus found in pig poo can cause environmental damage, so scientists developed **'Enviropig',** a pig that produces less phosphorus in its poo.
#0510

The **Tasmanian tiger** became extinct in the 1930s but scientists have **used remains** from a specimen to try and recreate tiny cells.
#0511

Mercury is a **poisonous metal.** In the early 21st century, American scientists developed **poplar trees** that could suck up mercury from contaminated soil through their roots.
#0512

British scientists have produced a **breed of hen** that lays eggs with cancer-fighting properties.
#0513

In 1993, scientists developed **goats** that could produce a **spider silk** protein in their milk. They used these animals to manufacture a very strong material called **biosteel.**
#0515

In 1951, scientists discovered that cells taken from cancer patient **Henrietta Lacks** could be kept alive and made to multiply. They were named HeLa...
#0514

...HeLa cells have been used for research into **cancer, AIDS,** toxic substances, and many other areas.
#0516

Trees are being genetically altered to grow faster and withstand biological attacks.
#0517

Scientists have developed **bananas** that can carry vaccines. Instead of having an injection, you just eat a banana to protect yourself from diseases.
#0518

**Cow farts** are a major contributor to global warming. So scientists in America have bred a cow that farts **25 per cent less** than normal cows.
#0519

# 5 filthy facts about the VIRTUAL WORLD

There are more devices connected to the Internet than there are **people on the entire planet.** #0520

Of the 6 billion people living on Earth in 2012, 4.8 billion had a mobile phone but only **4.2 billion owned a toothbrush.** #0521

**400 million people** around the world play **MMO** (Massively Multiplayer Online) video games, spending £8 billion in 2012, more than the USA spends on **cosmetics in a year.** #0522

In total, gamers have spent the equivalent of **200,000 years** playing **Angry Birds,** approximately the same amount of time that **humans have existed.** #0523

More than half of smartphone owners check their Facebook page before they get **out of bed** in the morning, and one third will read it **on the toilet.** #0524

# 8 gross computer facts

**SPIDER** infestations, **mice, cockroaches** and even **dead lizards** have been found inside home PCs. #0525

It takes **244 kg** of **fossil fuel, 22 kg** of **chemicals** and **1.5 tonnes** of **water** to manufacture **one computer**. #0526

DRY EYES ARE A COMMON PROBLEM for computer users because the average person only blinks **7 TIMES PER MINUTE** when using a computer – less than half the normal amount. #0527

120

An estimated **50 million tonnes** of

# W.E.E.E.

(Waste Electrical and Electronic Equipment) are produced each year – that's the equivalent of **100 fully laden oil tankers.**

#0528

An average 21-year-old has spent **5000 hours playing video games.** They have also sent 250,000 emails, instant messages and texts, spent 10,000 hours on a mobile phone, and picked their nose 30,000 times.

#0530

Computers are getting smaller, more powerful and more portable. **Google** has made a **wearable** computer, in the form of voice-activated **glasses.**

#0529

# SINCE 1997,

it has been possible to have a computer **implanted in your brain** to help control neural diseases, such as **epilepsy.**

#0531

# 100 million
**phones are disposed** of in Europe **each year** – that's more than the **combined populations** of Germany and Romania.

#0532

# 11 CRAZY ROBOT FACTS

First released in 2004, the **'robosapien'** was a toy robot that was built to behave like a human, even making **farting and belching sounds.**

#0533

Kobe Airport in Japan has a robot called **DCBA** that can clean a urinal in 10 seconds. #0534

A **robot toilet** at Frankfurt Airport in Germany has its own arm that **sprays water** at the toilet bowl to clean it. #0535

In 2005, a UK scientist began developing an **Ecobot** that will be powered by **bacteria from rotting apples and dead flies.**

#0536

In his 2000 book *Robot*, Hans Moravec predicts that robots will be able to match human intelligence by 2040 and by 2050 they will be smarter.

#0537

Since 2000, the da Vinci robotic surgical system has been **helping surgeons** perform minor operations.

#0538

The Mondo Spider is a 725-kg, 8-legged, solar-powered **walking machine** originally built in 2006.

#0539

Developed in 2012, **Kenji the robot** was programmed to **fall in 'love'**. Unfortunately Kenji fell in love with anyone he 'saw' and liked to give them **bone-crushing 'hugs'**.

#0540

Future robots might be as small as **100 nanometres** (100 billionths of a metre) or 1000 times smaller than the width of a human hair...

#0541

...These tiny robots would be **small enough to explore the inside of a blood cell** and provide medical treatment.

#0542

The **iRobot Scooba** is built to scrub the smallest, dirtiest nooks and crannies, such as behind your toilet.

#0543

# 11 FREAKY FACTS ABOUT SPACE EXPLORATION

If you **farted** in a spacesuit, the **smell would stay inside.**
#0544

In 1961, Alan Shepard, the first American in space, realized that he needed to pee during his mission – but there was **no toilet!** So he peed **in his spacesuit!** #0545

Today, astronauts often wear **special nappies** during lift-off, re-entry and on space walks. #0546

124

**Before going into space, astronauts have to train on a special zero-gravity toilet simulator.** #0547

There are more than 500,000 pieces of **space junk** orbiting Earth.

#0548

With little gravity in space, the liquids in your body move up towards your head, **filling your nose with snot.** #0549

If a **frog vomited in space,** the zero gravity would make it **throw up its stomach as well.**

#0550

Some astronauts have reported that there is a **meaty-metallic smell** in space. While others report a **rum and raspberry smell.**

#0551

Almost half of all astronauts suffer from **'space sickness',** and zero-gravity vomit is hard to clean up!

#0552

**Space poo** has to be sucked away, freeze-dried and then stored to stop it from **floating around.** #0553

Sometimes, the bits of **freeze-dried poo** have floated free of the toilet, and astronauts have **caught them in their mouths** thinking they were **peanuts.** #0554

# 6 facts about Other Planets

Because of the **stronger gravity,** you would be **27 times heavier** on the Sun than on Earth (and a lot warmer). So if you weigh **100 kg** on Earth, you would weigh nearly **3 tonnes** on the surface of the Sun. #0555

Venus has 350-km/h winds, a permanent toxic smog that traps heat close to the ground, and a surface **temperature of 450°C.** #0556

**The rain on Venus is**

# sulphuric acid...

...It would dissolve anything it touched – your spaceship, your umbrella AND YOU.

#0557

Venus and Mars have atmospheres that are almost entirely made up of **CARBON DIOXIDE**. Breathing the air there would lead to **unconsciousness and then death**.

#0558

Jupiter, Saturn, Uranus and Neptune are **giant balls of stinking gases** such as METHANE AND AMMONIA. Under the **thick layer of gas** is **liquid methane and ammonia**.

#0559

A storm on Mars can whip up a thick red

## dust cloud

that can blanket the planet for **months.**

#0560

**Before the storm**     **After the storm**

127

# 5 REPELLENT PLANET

The Yellow River in China is the muddiest in the world, with **2 billion tonnes** of **yellow mud** flowing down it every year. #0561

# 11 facts about Rainforests

A mother **slow loris** licks her babies with her **poisonous saliva** to protect them from predators. #0562

Some **piranha fish** in the River Amazon attack in groups, **ripping the flesh off their prey.** #0563

Up until the early 20th century, rainforest **headhunters** killed intruders by **cutting off their heads.** They then boiled the heads, and **kept them as trophies.** #0564

**Every second, an area of rainforest the size of a football pitch is cut down.** #0565

The Amazon gets **2.7 m of rain** every year – that's about the distance from your bedroom floor to the ceiling. #0566

The **cowitch tropical plant** has leaves with poisonous hairs that cause **extreme itchiness** on contact... #0567

...One of the best ways to cure the itching is to **rub in cow dung!** #0568

The world's **largest snake** is the Amazonian common anaconda, which grows up to **9 m long** (about the same as the height of a giraffe). #0571

The rainforest is so dense that the floor receives only **2 per cent of the sunlight that reaches the tops of the trees.** As a result, it is home to fungi, **decaying plant and animal matter and lots of insects.** #0572

**Bullet ants** grow to the size of your little finger, and deliver a **sting so powerful** that it feels like you've been hit by **a bullet.** #0569

**Electric eels,** found in rainforest rivers, can **shock** you with hundreds of volts of electricity. #0570

# 8 DEADLY DESERT FACTS

Deserts are places where **less than 25 cm of rain** falls in a year. In July 1956, Unionville, USA, got **more than that in a single minute!**

#0573

The **deathstalker scorpion** likes to crawl into travellers' tents. A **bite** from this venomous critter can cause **months of pain,** and even **DEATH.**

#0574

The **Gila monster,** a biting lizard, lives in the Mexican desert. It is **highly poisonous,** but it moves so slowly that it is not a great danger to humans.

#0575

A camel can shut its nose to keep out desert sand.

#0576

# A cactus plant's

**dagger-sharp spines** store water in the dry desert and also ensure that any hungry herbivore would think twice before munching on them.

#0577

The kangaroo rat's **pee** comes out in the form of a **PASTE** so that it does not lose water.

#0578

Desert-dwelling **dung beetles collect balls of poo,** which they roll around and store as food.

#0579

**Sheep's eyes are a delicacy** in the north African desert. They are usually boiled up with the rest of the head, and offered as **TREATS**.

#0580

# 8 CHILLY POLAR FACTS

**Male musk oxen** are among the SMELLIEST CREATURES in the Arctic tundra. They release a **strong odour during mating season** to attract females, and they also like to mark their territory with **wee.**

#0581

In 1898, the ship **BELGICA** got stuck in the ice during an expedition to Antarctica. When the food ran out, the crew had to **eat penguins and seals.**

#0582

Scientists who visit Antarctica have to **take home all their rubbish, including wee and poo.** #0583

Polar bears **HUNT SEALS,** biting into their heads to kill them.

#0584

In the freezing Arctic, extremities such as fingers and toes can suffer from **frostbite,** where the skin becomes **black** and **blistered.**

#0585

Frostbite can be treated by carefully re-heating the body. However, if the damage is too severe, the infected area may have to be **AMPUTATED.**

#0586

Polar explorers who don't wear protective goggles suffer from **snow blindness** when the strong UV light damages their eyes. It's a bit like having **sunburnt eyes!**

#0587

The lion's mane jellyfish has **POISONOUS TENTACLES** that can trail up to **36 m** – longer than a tennis court.

#0588

135

# 12 Grisly Mountain facts

Mountain climbing is the **second most dangerous** sport in the world (the first is cave diving). #0589

When a passenger plane crashed in the Andes in 1972, the survivors stayed alive by **eating those who had died.** #0590

More than **40 bodies** have been found **frozen** on the climb up Mount Everest. #0591

Mount Everest is covered in rubbish, including discarded ropes and **piles of human poo...** #0592

...In 2000, guides found over **600 discarded oxygen bottles** on Everest. #0593

136

High up, low air pressure causes body changes that lead to **altitude sickness,** which can make you tired, dizzy and nauseous. #0594

Local guides around Everest think the best way to get rid of altitude sickness is eating **stinky garlic soup.** #0595

**A 4000-m peak** in the Swiss Alps called the **Eiger** is known as **'the murderous wall'** for its **dangerous climb.** #0596

In 1924, British mountaineer George Mallory disappeared on Everest. His body was found in 1999 at 8200 m. He hadn't made it to the top. #0599

K2 in the Himalayas is called the **'savage mountain'.** One in four people who make it to the top **don't make it back down.** #0597

Some of the ice on Mont Blanc, France, is so **polluted by pee** that it has turned yellow. #0598

In 1995, **a 500-year-old frozen mummy** of a young girl was found near the top of Mount Ampato in southern Peru. #0600

137

# 11 **facts** about OCEANS

A **3000-passenger** cruise liner generates about **8 tonnes of solid waste** per week. #0601

Swirling currents called **gyres** can appear in the ocean. These whirling currents can trap large amounts of **rubbish**.
#0602

When waves break on parts of the shore, the water is pushed in **different directions** until it is forced back out towards the sea. The resulting **rip currents** can be **DEADLY.** #0603

In 2010, **five million barrels of oil were spilled** into the Gulf of Mexico, polluting thousands of square kilometres of water. #0604

In the South Pacific, there are more than **1100 active volcanoes under water.** #0605

**Dive deeper**

than 1 km into the ocean and you enter **the midnight zone**. It is pitch black, apart from a few **luminous animals.** #0606

Vents on the ocean floor pour out super-heated chemicals and gases… #0607

…**Bizarre life forms surround the vents**, including giant tubeworms, giant clams and blind fish. #0608

Some underwater volcanoes **spew stinky methane and mud** instead of lava. #0609

Some little organisms feed entirely on the chemicals spewed out by underwater volcanoes. #0610

If you swallow ocean water, you'll also swallow **millions of viruses and bacteria.** #0611

# 11 foul facts about RIVERS

About **1 billion litres of raw sewage** is dumped into the Ganges River in India and Bangladesh every day. #0613

**40 per cent** of the USA's rivers are too polluted for fishing, swimming or to sustain aquatic life. #0612

> **However, many of the 420 million people** who live near the Ganges rely on the water for washing and drinking. #0614

Bacteria levels in the Ganges are **3000 times** above the level that is considered safe. #0615

More than half of the world's **500 major rivers** are badly polluted. #0616

Found in the River Amazon, anacondas eat fish, birds, mammals and other reptiles. Sometimes, **hungry females even eat males.** #0617

If you **wee** in the River Nile, Egypt, **parasitic worms could find their way into your body** by following the warm pee trail. #0618

**Up to a third of male fish in UK rivers** are in the process of changing sex due to pollution, specifically the female hormones found in human sewage. #0619

**In 1858, the smell of raw sewage from the River Thames in the UK** was so bad that Parliament was dissolved. **It was known as the 'GREAT STINK'.** #0620

The River Congo in West Central Africa is the **world's most dangerous river.** Rapids surge through a **120-km impassable canyon** known as the **Gates of Hell.** #0621

The aggressive **BULL SHARK** swims up freshwater rivers and **attacks prey** in shallow water. #0622

141

# 10 Wicked Weather facts

The 1815 eruption of **Mount Tambora,** Indonesia, threw out so much dust that the sun was blotted out. Temperatures around the world fell, and there was no summer in Europe that year. #0623

If a cloud is so low to the ground that it's impossible to tell where snow-covered land ends and the cloud begins, you are in a **whiteout.** #0624

Russians joke that their greatest weapon is **'General Winter'.** The severe Russian winter has frozen the guns and troops of several invading armies. #0625

Each year, there are about **10,000 big thunderstorms** and **1000 tornadoes and hurricanes** in the USA. #0626

142

In 1955, a girl riding a horse in South Dakota, USA, was **sucked inside a tornado**. Both the horse and the girl landed safely after travelling **more than a kilometre** in the air.

#0627

The deadliest single tornado was the 'Tri-state' tornado that **killed 695 people** in Missouri, Illinois and Indiana in March 1925.

#0628

Falling air pressure can create a violent wind known as a 'bomb'. In 1987, a 'bomb' flattened **15 million trees** in England.

#0629

The temperature of a lightning bolt can reach **30,000°C.**

#0630

Lightning strikes somewhere on Earth about **100 times every second.**

#0631

In the USA, about **50 people** a year are **struck dead** by a bolt of lightning.

#0632

# 7 facts about dirty Beaches

Shellfish such as mussels filter out **raw sewage** from water and eat it. #0633

The smell of the seaside is caused by **slimy rotting seaweed** trapped under sand or rocks. #0634

In 2007, volunteers picked up **3000 tonnes of rubbish** across 76 countries – that is as heavy as **600 elephants.** #0635

In 2008, an unknown beast called the **'Montauk monster'** was washed up on a New York beach. Scientists still haven't been able to identify it. #0636

In 2011, **6000 dead ducks and gulls** washed up on a Canadian beach after eating contaminated fish. #0637

In 2012, a **fish eye the size of a tennis ball** was found on a beach in Florida. No one is sure what species it came from. #0638

The white sand on coral beaches contains lots of **parrotfish poo.** #0639

# 9 facts about hot and cold

**At -44°C,** human flesh freezes in about 1 minute.

#0640

When you get REALLY COLD, **your blood pressure rises** as blood vessels constrict to reduce heat loss. In response, your kidneys get rid of fluid to lower your blood pressure again, making you want to **pee more.**

#0641

If you don't wear **goggles** in **high-wind-chill conditions,** the **corneas** of your eyes can freeze.

#0642

**Miliaria**

**or 'prickly heat'** can happen when you **sweat too much** in hot weather, causing an **itchy, stinging rash.**

#0644

**Heat oedema** is the pooling of fluids under the skin in **extreme heat,** causing **hands or legs** to SWELL UP.

#0643

On 10 July 1913, temperatures in **Death Valley, California,** were recorded at **57°C** in the shade – **the hottest ever.**

#0645

**Sunburn** actually **DAMAGES YOUR DNA,** destroying skin cells, which is why you peel after a really bad burn.

#0646

Drinking too much water can cause low sodium in the blood, resulting in **vomiting, headaches, fatigue, cramps or even a coma.** It is known as **HYPONATREMIA.**

#0647

**Extreme heat** makes you **sweat lots,** which can lead to **dehydration.** This is known as **HYPERNATREMIA.**

#0648

147

# 12 soggy facts about Rain AND hail

Tornadoes and water spouts can pick up **SMALL ANIMALS.** Later, they rain back down to earth as frozen animal lumps.
#0649

In 1863, a farmer in Quebec, Canada, found a **frog** inside a large hailstone.
#0650

In 1873, **a storm of frogs** fell on the state of Missouri, USA.
#0652

In 2001, some mysterious red rain fell on Kerala, India. It took its colour from airborne fungal spores. #0651

The people of Tasmania, Australia, found a **SLIMY JELLIED RAIN** on their properties the morning after a big thunderstorm. It is believed to have been fish eggs or jellyfish. #0653

Fungal spores in soil release an **odour** that gives rainwater its distinctive smell. #0654

On 14 July 1953, **golf-ball-sized hailstones** fell in Alberta, Canada, **killing 36,000 ducks.** #0655

In 1890, **blood rained from the sky** in Calabria, Italy. The blood was thought to have come from birds killed by violent winds. #0656

A **shower of herring fish** fell on the town of Bournemouth, UK, in 1948. #0657

The **biggest hailstone** ever recorded was more than 20 cm wide — that's **bigger than a softball.** #0658

Some people are **allergic to rain,** and touching it causes swelling and redness. #0659

In 1976, a **gigantic flash flood** swept down the Big Thompson River Canyon in Colorado, USA, after three quarters of the area's annual rainfall fell in **just 4 hours.** #0660

# 10 FREEZING FACTS ABOUT SNOW

Thundersnow **is a BLIZZARD** that happens in a thunderstorm. Often **snow will fall** and **lightning will strike** at the same time.
#0661

A really bad **snowstorm** can dump more than **40 million tonnes** of snow over a large city. #0662

New York had 60 cm of snow during the winter of 2011. **Rat-infested sofas and rotten rubbish were found on the streets** after it melted. #0663

From **1998** to **1999, 30 m** of snow fell on Mount Baker, USA – enough to bury a ten-storey building. #0664

An **ARIZONA** snow resort filled its slopes with fake snow made entirely out of urine.

#0665

**Snow** gathers lots of **POLLUTION** and dirt from the air as it falls.

#0666

If you eat **snow** when you're stuck in a **blizzard,** it will make you **colder** and even more dehydrated.

#0668

Some algae can grow in settled snow,

#0667

making the snow change colour.

Dutchman Wim Hof **ran a half marathon barefoot** in the snow in 2 hours 16 minutes.

#0669

Some **SNOW ALGAE** is also known as WATERMELON SNOW, because it smells fruity and has a red tinge. However, eating it will make you **sick.**

#0670

151

# 9 facts about CLIMATE CHANGE

Ocean water is becoming **MORE ACIDIC** because of **increased carbon dioxide emissions.** This causes growth disorders in some marine animals.
#0671

**Warm oceans** cause coral to bleach, and eventually die. #0672

Past climate conditions can be worked out by **studying the remains of dead beetles** – different beetles lived in different climates. #0673

After the last Ice Age, seawater expanded and ice melted, causing **sea levels to rise by 130 m** – that's the height of a 40-storey building. #0674

**Global warming** is **causing water levels to rise.** Small island nations, such as Tuvalu in the Pacific, are in danger of disappearing altogether.
#0675

152

As the northern hemisphere gets warmer, **DISEASE-CARRYING PESTS** such as mosquitoes will move north. #0676

Scientists list 12 diseases called the **DEADLY DOZEN** that will spread because of climate change. These include yellow fever, cholera and bubonic plague. #0677

The rise in temperatures due to global warming will make people more susceptible to heat rashes and other skin complaints. #0678

**Methane** is a greenhouse gas, which traps radiated heat in the atmosphere, warming up the Earth. It can be generated by **cow dung** and **cow farts**. #0679

# 12 DISGUSTING DINOSAUR FACTS

Scientists have learned much about prehistoric life by studying **COPROLITES – fossilized dinosaur droppings.** #0680

Sometimes, dinosaurs would become trapped in **pits of gloopy tar and mud. The skeletons of these trapped animals** would then be preserved as **fossils.**
#0681

The **MILLIONS OF TONNES OF POO** made by dinosaurs every day made the ground fertile. #0682

**Little bits of bone** have been found in **TYRANNOSAURUS COPROLITES,** showing how they could crunch up the bones of their prey.
#0684

A huge **coprolite** made by a dinosaur called a Maiasaura, was found in Wyoming, USA. It was the **size** and **shape** of a **basketball.** #0683

The **preserved stomach contents** of dinosaurs have been found in some fossils. **The remains show diets ranging from seeds and plants to whole animals.** #0685

Sauropod dinosaurs would **swallow big stones** called **gastroliths** to help them digest food. #0686

A Tyrannosaurus rex could eat up to **23 KG OF MEAT** in one bite, which is the equivalent of more than **100 fillet steaks.** #0687

The world's oldest **FOSSILIZED VOMIT** was discovered in 2002. It was made by an ichthyosaur, a marine reptile that lived at the same time as the dinosaurs. #0689

The meat-eating theropod dinosaurs had **SERRATED, KNIFE-LIKE TEETH** to help them rip apart flesh. #0688

The **Irritator** was a big meat-eating spinosaur, so-named because a frustrated scientist had to spend hours piecing together its broken skull. #0690

Velociraptors had one long, **curved claw** on each of their hind legs, which they would use to slash at prey to make them bleed to death. #0691

155

# 11 facts about LIFE IN THE PAST

**Trilobites were ancient bugs** related to insects and spiders.

They had a **HARD skeleton** on the outside of their bodies, which they replaced in order to grow.

#0692

Underneath a trilobite's skeleton was a **squishy** body, with several parts moving freely to help them wriggle about. #0693

**350 million years ago,** the high levels of oxygen in the atmosphere allowed insects to grow larger than rats.

#0694

**Arthropleura** was a MONSTROUS MILLIPEDE that grew **3 m long** – longer than the diamondback rattlesnake.

#0695

Many species have died out in the **'mass extinction events'** that have occurred through history, in which MOST LIFE ON EARTH WAS WIPED OUT.

#0696

Dunkleosteus was a fish that **lived in the ocean 380–360 million years ago**. It was over **10 m long,** and had a ferocious bite.

#0697

The **giant dragonfly** meganeura had a wingspan of 76 cm – that's BIGGER THAN A PIGEON.

#0698

There have been several **VERY COLD PERIODS IN THE PAST 2 million** years, during which species died out, and new ones emerged.

#0699

Some mass **extinction events** were very sudden, such as the meteorite impact that wiped out the

dinosaurs

**65 million years ago...**

#0701

More than **650 MILLION YEARS AGO,** Earth froze over completely, and looked like a giant snowball.

#0700

...The explosion threw up so much **ash** that the sun was hidden, temperatures fell, and no large animal was **able to survive.**

#0702

# 6 GROSS

New York City is home to **8 million people** and ......

PEOPLE

**250,000 rats –**
that's 1 rat for every 36 people. #0703

# 13 GRIMY FACTS ABOUT CITIES

**Manila, the capital of the Philippines,** is so crowded that there are **41,014 people** crammed into each square kilometre, roughly **8 times** the density of London. #0704

In December 2005, air pollution was so bad in **Tehran, Iran,** that **1600 people were hospitalized.** #0705

**Air pollution** is a huge problem in **Mexico City** because it is in a valley. A **blanket of smog** caused by cars and factories is often visible over the city. #0706

**Traffic jams** in São Paulo, Brazil, are so bad that many people spend **five hours a day** driving to and from work. #0708

Urban foxes eat almost anything – **slugs, worms, rats...** #0707

...But a fox's favourite meal is whatever it can find in the nearest bin! #0709

**London** has more **urban foxes** than it does **buses.** #0710

The world's **hottest city** is **Bangkok, Thailand,** where the temperature never drops below a sticky **20°C day or night.**

#0711

Every day in
# Mumbai,
India, the city's trains carry six million people – that's the same as the whole population of Israel. #0712

## San Pedro Sula in Honduras
is so dangerous that in 2011, **1143 people** were murdered. That's more than **3 MURDERS** per day.

#0713

At least **30 per cent** of the drinking water in **Singapore** comes from **recycled water,** including some from **toilets.**

#0714

# Ulaanbaatar
in Mongolia is the **world's coldest capital city.** The temperature remains below freezing from November to March, and a 20-cm-thick layer of snow covers the city. #0715

## PYONGYANG, NORTH KOREA, has so many power cuts that many people avoid the metro train in case they get trapped underground.

#0716

# 9 facts about RUBBISH

Mumbai, India, gets rid of the horrid smell of its rubbish tip by pouring **thousands of litres of deodorant on it.** #0717

The **Citarum River** in Indonesia is filled with the rubbish of **9 million people,** plus the liquid waste of **500 factories...** #0718

...In places, the water can no longer be seen beneath the moving carpet of rubbish... #0719

...Boatmen still go on the river, but not to fish. **They look for things in the rubbish to sell.** #0720

The Pacific is home to the **Great Pacific Rubbish Patch,** a vast soup of debris and chemical sludge that covers about **5000 km².**
#0721

About **6.3 billion kg of rubbish** is dumped into the oceans every year, **most of it plastic.**
#0722

When rubbish decomposes in a landfill, it produces methane gas – that's the smelly gas **in farts.**
#0723

In a landfill, cigarette butts take 12 years to biodegrade. **'Disposable' nappies take 800 years** to biodegrade.
#0724

Until the early 20th century, thrown-out food was mixed with **animal remains** to make a greasy gunk used in soaps and candles.
#0725

163

# 9 facts about POLLUTION

**Linfen, China,** is one of the most polluted cities on the planet due to the coal dust produced by the city's mines...

#0726

In Ranipet, India, the **water in local rivers is SO TOXIC** that it **feels like an insect bite** when it touches the skin.

#0727

...In fact, 16 of the world's 20 most polluted cities are in **China.**

#0728

Over **1 BILLION people in the world** do not have access to **clean drinking water** and **5000 people die** each day due to **dirty drinking water.**

#0729

164

Some oceans have **dead zones** – nothing can live there because pollution has caused an **oxygen shortage.** #0730

If you see **COTTON BUDS** on a beach, DON'T SWIM THERE. People flush them down the loo, so they're a sign that **untreated poo has flowed into the water.** #0731

**LONDON** was once so THICKLY POLLUTED with coal smoke that it created a thick fog known as a **'pea souper'.** #0732

**Swimming and fishing are banned** in Onondago Lake, New York State, USA, because it has so much **sewage and industrial waste.** #0733

The **ACROPOLIS** is a collection of ruined buildings in Athens, Greece. Acid rain has caused these old buildings to **crumble** more **in the last 40 years** than they did in the previous 2500. #0734

# 11 facts about yucky FESTIVALS

In the Rattlesnake roundup in Sweetwater, Texas, **contestants take part in a rattlesnake-eating contest.** #0735

At Thorrablot, a midwinter feast in Iceland, **seal flippers** and **rotting shark** meat are served. #0736

In the **Blobfest** of Pennsylvania, USA, the crowd re-enact scenes from the old horror movie, *The Blob.* #0737

During the Interstate Mullet Toss in the USA, **mullet fish are thrown over the state line** between Alabama and Florida. #0738

Every year in July, people try to **outrun a group of bulls** through the **streets of Pamplona,** Spain, to prove their bravery. Up to **300 PEOPLE** are injured every time. #0739

**THE WORLD BOG SNORKELLING CHAMPIONSHIP,** held in Wales, UK, has contestants snorkelling through deep puddles of sludge. #0740

In the town of Ivrea, Italy, rival teams **throw oranges at each other** during the BATTLE OF THE ORANGES, which is held every February. #0741

Every year in Thailand, people present fruit and vegetables to the local monkey population at the **Monkey** **Buffet Festival.** #0742

In spring, Hindus throw coloured paint at each other during the festival of **Holi.** #0743

In Mali, there's a **mud-plastering festival** each spring, when everyone **slaps mud** on the buildings and themselves. #0744

In August, **Spaniards do battle** in the world's biggest **tomato fight,** known as **La Tomatina,** on the streets of **Buñol, Valencia.** #0745

167

# 8 grim facts about BUILDINGS

**Poo** mixed with **straw** is used to make bricks in some countries. #0746

The ancient Egyptian pyramids were actually **tombs,** built to hold the **mummified bodies** of the pharaohs (kings). #0747

In tropical countries, the tiny **pharaoh ant** is a major pest in hospitals and offices. They breed huge colonies in **between sheets of paper!** #0748

The stones in an African rondavel (a type of house) are stuck together USING COW POO. #0749

Wembley Stadium in the UK has **2618 toilets,** more than any other venue in the world. #0750

Poor airflow, mould and toxic paint can cause 'Sick Building Syndrome' (SBS). #0751

SBS has a variety of symptoms including **headaches, nausea, throat irritation, a runny nose and skin rashes.** #0752

In New York, a kids' playground was built out of pure steel. **The steel heated to 52°C** in summer and kids couldn't play there. #0753

169

# 10 stinky facts about FARMING

Before the invention of chemical fertilizers, farmers' fields were fertilized with **animal dung** and **human poo.** #0754

A third of all the fruit and vegetables we eat contain chemical pesticides

## SPRAYED ON THE FIELDS

where they were grown.

#0755

There are more than **50 BILLION** chickens in the world – outnumbering people by more than 7 to 1. #0756

Each day, the world's chickens produce **poo** that totals the equivalent weight of **50 aircraft carriers.** #0757

In Wales, UK, there are
# THREE TIMES
more sheep than people.
#0758

**HAGGIS**
is a traditional dish in Scotland. It is made of minced sheep **heart, liver** and **lungs,** and wrapped in the lining of the sheep's **stomach.** #0760

**MUTTON BUSTING** is a popular sport in some US rodeo shows – children ride **sheep** instead of **bulls.** #0759

Dairy cows provide
# 90%
of the world's milk supply.
The best cows provide more than 25 l of milk per day – that's **100** glasses of milk!
#0761

A cow could walk up some stairs, but would have trouble walking down again – its knees don't **BEND THE RIGHT WAY.** #0762

There are around **1 billion pigs** in the world, and half of them live in **CHINA.** #0763

# 11 facts about SEWERS

In Victorian London, **HUMAN SEWAGE** drained into the River Thames, turning the **drinking water brown.**

#0764

In Mexico City in 2000, heavy rain broke down the wall of a sewage canal. **Thousands of homes were flooded 1 m high with sewage.**

#0765

In 1848, a law was passed in the UK stating that all houses should have an **ash pit, where poo and wee fell into a pile of ash** ready for collection.

#0766

London built a modern sewer system after the **'GREAT STINK' OF 1858 WHEN A SMELL OF POO** hung over the city.

#0767

Toilet paper was first used in **China** more than **1500 years ago.**

#0768

Before toilet paper was widely available, rich people used **wool, lace** or **hemp** to wipe their bottoms, while the poor used **rags, leaves, sand or their hands.**

#0769

The average person will go to the toilet about **2500** times a year and spend **3 years** on the loo in their lifetime!

#0770

The toilet nearest the entrance in a public toilet is **likely to be the cleanest** because it is used least often.

#0771

If you use a composting toilet, micro-organisms **break down the sewage into compost.**

#0772

In New South Wales, Australia, so many **frogs invaded the public toilets** that the toilets stopped working.

#0773

Rats are good underwater swimmers and can swim up pipes and **INTO YOUR TOILET.**

#0774

# 11 rotten facts about LIFE ON SHIP

Ship's biscuits, known as **HARDTACK,** were eaten by sailors from the 16th century. They were baked up to **6 months** in advance of a voyage and could last for many years…

#0775

…The biscuits were so **HARD** that they were said to be able to stop a **bullet.**

#0776

The maiden voyage of the **TITANIC** was very **smelly.** More than 700 third-class passengers had **two bathtubs** between them.

#0777

**Weevils and maggots** were fond of hardtack so sailors tapped their biscuits to get rid of any **creepy crawlies.**

#0778

Sailors who fell asleep on duty or **did a poo** onboard instead of overboard could be **disciplined.**

#0779

The most severe discipline was to be lashed by the **CAT-O'-NINE-TAILS** – a multi-tailed whip. #0780

After the punishment, the wounds were washed with **seawater** to prevent infection, but this caused **EXTRA PAIN.** #0781

In the early 19th century, convicts were shipped to **Australia.** Conditions were so terrible that many died on the journey, which took up to **six months.** #0782

Convicts were kept below deck in chains most of the time and got very seasick. The galleys were

# A WASH WITH VOMIT.

#0783

By the time they arrived, many had **TYPHOID AND CHOLERA,** or were weakened by **SCURVY, DYSENTERY OR FEVER.** #0784

Today, about **60** large ships sink or run aground every day. #0785

# 13 FREAKY FLYING FACTS

In the 16th century, Italian **Paolo Guidotti made wings from whalebone and feathers** and attempted to fly. He fell through the roof of a church and broke his leg. #0786

In 1928, wealthy businessman Alfred Lowenstein mistook the door of his aeroplane for the toilet and plunged **1220 m** into the English Channel. #0787

**Mid-air panic** was caused by a Sri Lankan cricketer in 2013 when he tried **to open the door** of an aeroplane thinking it was the toilet. #0788

Pre-packed airline food often tastes bland. That's because the aircraft's **noise distracts your senses** from noticing taste. #0789

Airline tea tastes funny because the cabin pressure means the **water boils at 90°C instead of 100°C** – not hot enough to make a decent brew. #0790

In January 2009, a US passenger flight had to make an emergency landing on the Hudson River when a **flock of geese flew into both engines...** #0791

**...All 155 passengers and crew survived,**
# BUT THE GEESE DID NOT. #0792

**Niek Vermeulen from the Netherlands has the world's largest collection of airline sick bags...** #0793

...He's collected 6016 **'BARF BAGS'** from
# 1142
**different airlines.** #0794

Toilet waste is stored in a huge
# TANK
inside the plane and sucked out at the end of a flight. #0795

In 2004, Virgin Atlantic introduced **Design for Chunks,** a competition to design sick bags. #0796

In 2013, a British woman found a frozen block of airline poo and wee that had crashed into her house. #0797

In 2013, passengers on a 13-hour flight suffered from a **violent vomiting** and **diarrhoea bug** – and there were only four toilets on the plane. #0798

**177**

# 7 foul facts about Railways

The earliest passenger trains in the UK had three classes of travel – first and second class were comfortable carriages, but third-class passengers had to ride in **open-top** goods wagons, seated on **wooden benches.** #0799

US steam locomotives were fitted with a V-shaped device at the front. They were known as **cowcatchers** and were designed to push away obstacles on the track, such as cows. #0800

Indian Railways carry more than **25 million passengers** every day, which is the same as the populations of Norway and Greece combined. #0801

People often leave strange things on trains. In 2009, **a dead octopus** was handed into Edinburgh Waverley station in the UK. #0802

In 2011, four bags of **VENOMOUS COBRAS** were left on a passenger train in Vietnam. #0803

**Waste** from train toilets is usually **flushed straight onto the tracks.** #0804

16 per cent of Dutch trains **do not have toilets** so in 2011 Dutch National Railways introduced **'WEE BAGS'.** In a toilet emergency, commuters can request one of the special plastic bags from the train conductor. #0805

179

# 11 CHOKING FACTS ABOUT CARS

**16% of car** owners never wash their cars.
#0806

The first pedestrian ever killed by a car was a British woman named Bridget Driscoll, in 1896. **She was struck by a car** that was travelling at just **6 KM/H.**
#0807

Driving motor vehicles releases more **AIR POLLUTION** than any other **human activity.**
#0808

'DIRTIER' cars emit their own weight in carbon gases **every six weeks.**
#0809

**In 2009, spindle ermine caterpillars span a silk COCOON** around a car to protect themselves while they **transformed into butterflies.** #0810

Alternative car fuels being tested include **sawdust, nuts, used nappies, chocolate, cow poo** and **turkey guts.** #0811

**In 2008, a US plastic surgeon claimed to have turned fat drained from his patients into biofuel.** #0812

Some people are experimenting with waste vegetable oil **(WVO)** or chip fat as a cleaner fuel for cars! #0813

In 2010, the Bio-Bug car made its debut. It runs on biogas produced by **HUMAN WASTE!** #0814

The kea, an alpine parrot native to New Zealand, **likes to nibble on cars.** #0815

In 2005, a British company launched the Indipod, an **in-car toilet.** #0816

# 8 scary facts about Schools

In Victorian England, teachers often punished pupils by **beating them with a cane...** #0817

...Boys were usually caned on their **backsides**... #0818

...Girls were either beaten on their **bare legs** or across their **hands.** #0819

**'Punishment baskets'** were used in some Victorian classrooms to suspend **badly behaved children** from the ceiling. #0820

Pupils who were slow learners had to wear a pointy **'dunce's cap'** or donkey's ears. #0821

School food is famously bad – one of the worst dishes was **'turkey twizzlers'**, which contained **only 34 per cent** turkey. The rest was mostly grain. #0822

Many kids become **anxious, frightened** or **nauseous** about going to school. This is called

# didaskaleinophobia or scolionophobia.

#0823

In ancient Sparta, 7-year-old boys at military school slept on beds of **sharp reeds** to get them used to pain. #0824

# 5 facts about PRISONS

In some old prisons, there is no toilet in a cell, so inmates have to use a bucket. Every morning, they have to **'SLOP OUT'** and carry their own waste to the drains.

#0825

Rikers Island Prison in New York is the **world's largest** prison, occupying a 1.6 km$^2$ site – the equivalent in size to **320 White Houses.**

#0826

The USA has the world's **biggest** prisoner population – **716 prisoners per 100,000 people.**

#0827

The **smallest** prisoner population is in the city state of San Marino, Italy, which had only **one prisoner** in 2011.

#0828

Victorian prisoners ate a **VERY BORING DIET** – they usually ate porridge for breakfast, soup for lunch, and porridge for dinner.

#0829

# 11 GROSS FACTS ABOUT HOMES

Every time you flush the loo, **you send an invisible 2-m plume of bacteria** into the air that lands on exposed surfaces.

#0830

**The toilet is not the dirtiest place in the bathroom,** IT'S THE SINK. The sink has **20,000 germs** per square centimere, but the toilet seat only has **20 germs per square centimetre.**

#0831

Locals in Florida, USA, found that **Cuban tree frogs** had swum up their pipes into their toilet bowls.

#0832

A kitchen chopping board has **200 per cent** more bacteria than the average **toilet seat.** #0833

Mice can squeeze through **cracks as small as 6 mm** to get into your house, and nest under the floor. #0834

Brown rat droppings are like mouse poo, but **three times larger.** #0835

Mouse droppings are easy to identify because they are **6 mm long, black** and **shaped like grains of rice.** #0836

**Black rat** droppings are more **sausage-shaped,** and look like fatter jelly beans. #0837

Bat droppings look like mouse droppings but are **shiny, speckled** and **always found in a pile.** #0838

**COCKROACH POO** looks like small dark specks. #0839

#0840

**Bird poo** contains **acid,** which eats into house bricks and damages them.

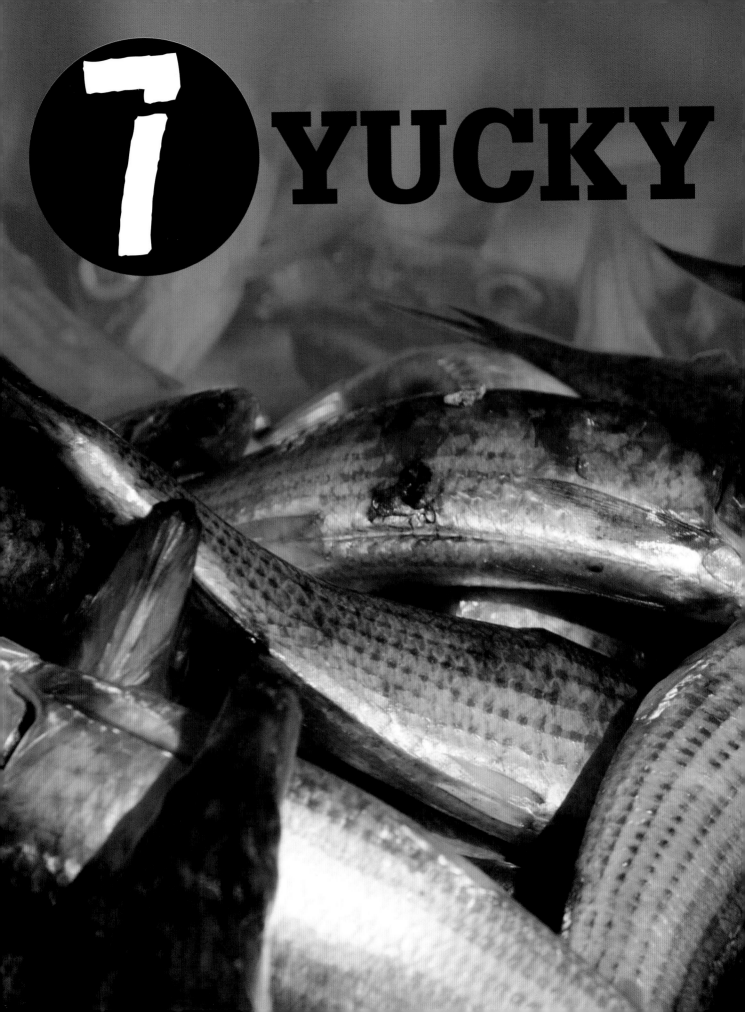

# 7 YUCKY

# FOOD

Garum was the ancient Romans' and Greeks' favourite sauce...

#0841

...It was made from **ROTTEN FISH.**

#0842

# 14 FACTS ABOUT EATING INSECTS

## More than 1900 SPECIES OF INSECT are eaten around the world. #0843

Fried locusts are a Nigerian delicacy. They taste a bit like prawns. #0844

Japanese athletes drink GIANT HORNET JUICE. This is a sports drink made from the stomach juices of **giant hornet larvae.** #0845

In Cambodia, **large spiders fried with garlic are a popular dish.** #0846

American Indians ROAST BEETLES and eat them like popcorn. #0848

People in Bali, Indonesia, catch **dragonflies** with a stick coated in sticky plant juice, grill them and then eat them. #0847

Food markets in Beijing, China, offer **candied scorpions on a stick.** #0849

Japanese restaurants may offer boiled **wasp larvae** or fried **SILK MOTH PUPAE.** #0850

# Thousands
**of Bogong moths return to the**
Bogong mountains
of Australia to breed every year, where people gather them up and eat them. #0851

The **witchetty grub** is a white moth **larva** the size of a **large finger** – it is a favourite food of Aboriginal Australians. #0852

In Mexico, **chapulines** are **grasshoppers** that are toasted with
# CHILLI
or garlic. #0853

In Laos, people eat **red ants** with egg tossed in a salad. #0854

In 2012, Dutch university professor Marcel Dicke published *The Insect Cookbook.*

He wanted to show people that insects can be a tasty source of protein. #0855

In 2013, a group of London art students **opened a restaurant** specializing in insects. Dishes included **watermelon** with **caterpillar risotto** and **ground-up cricket.** #0856

# 12 FOOD-EATING RECORD facts

Roman Emperor Nero started eating **dinner** in the **afternoon** and finished around **dawn.** The food included jellyfish, boiled tree fungi and flamingo.

#0857

In 2006, Japanese eating champion Takeru Kobayashi ate **97 HAMBURGERS** in **10 minutes,** beating his own world record by 28.

#0858

**Every day, Americans consume about 20 million hamburgers** and 9 million pizzas.

#0859

American Joey Chestnut is a world champion competitive eater. **In 2013, he beat his own record by scoffing**

# 69 HOT DOGS IN 10 MINUTES.

#0860

**Sumo wrestlers** eat two giant pots of meat stew every day to make sure they're heavy enough to fight.

#0861

For breakfast, Olympic swimmer Michael Phelps ate **three fried-egg sandwiches, a five-egg omelette, toast topped with sugar, and three pancakes.** For lunch, he ate **a huge bowl of pasta.** #0862

American Tim Janus can put away **140 PIECES OF SUSHI, in 6 minutes.** #0863

The largest number of **oysters swallowed in 3 minutes is 233.** #0864

**Korean-American Sonya Thomas** holds 20 food-eating records. One record involved eating

**44 LOBSTERS** in 12 minutes. #0867

Gary Bashaw Junior once mixed milk and chocolate powder in his mouth, then squirted 50 g of milkshake out of his nose. #0865

Over a **BILLION PEOPLE** around the world **are overweight,** which is about the same number as those who are made **ill from hunger.** #0866

American Don Lerman ate **seven 100 g sticks of salted butter** in 5 minutes. #0868

193

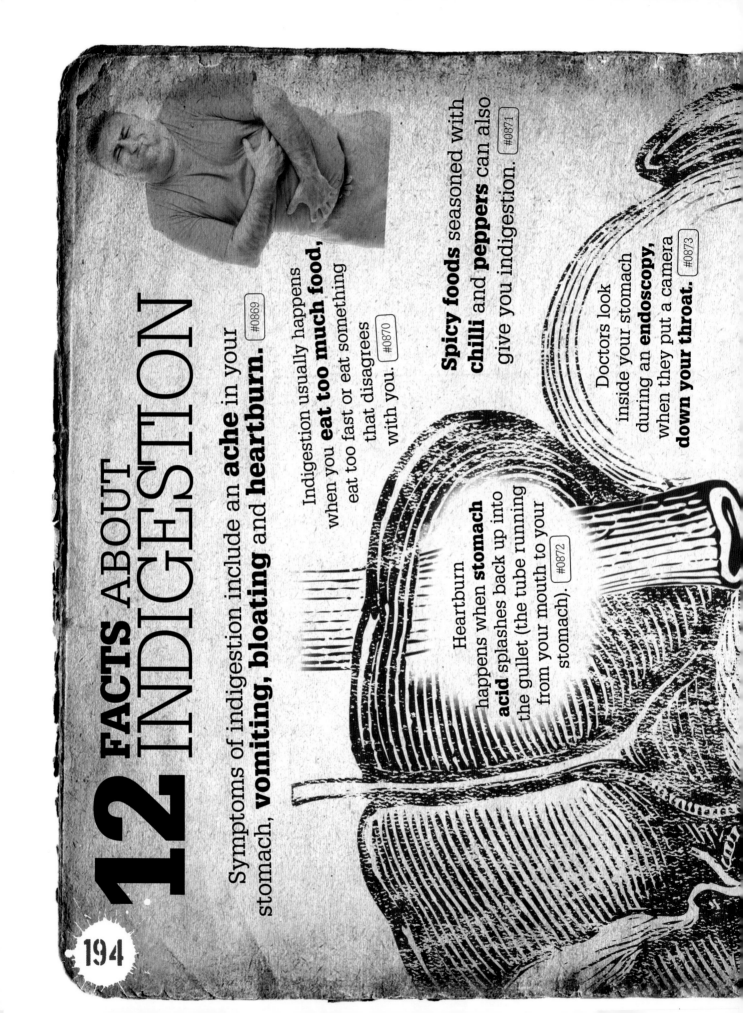

# 12 FACTS ABOUT INDIGESTION

Symptoms of indigestion include an **ache** in your stomach, **vomiting, bloating** and **heartburn.** #0869

Indigestion usually happens when you **eat too much food,** eat too fast or eat something that disagrees with you. #0870

**Spicy foods** seasoned with **chilli** and **peppers** can also give you indigestion. #0871

Heartburn happens when **stomach acid** splashes back up into the gullet (the tube running from your mouth to your stomach). #0872

Doctors look inside your stomach during an **endoscopy,** when they put a camera **down your throat.** #0873

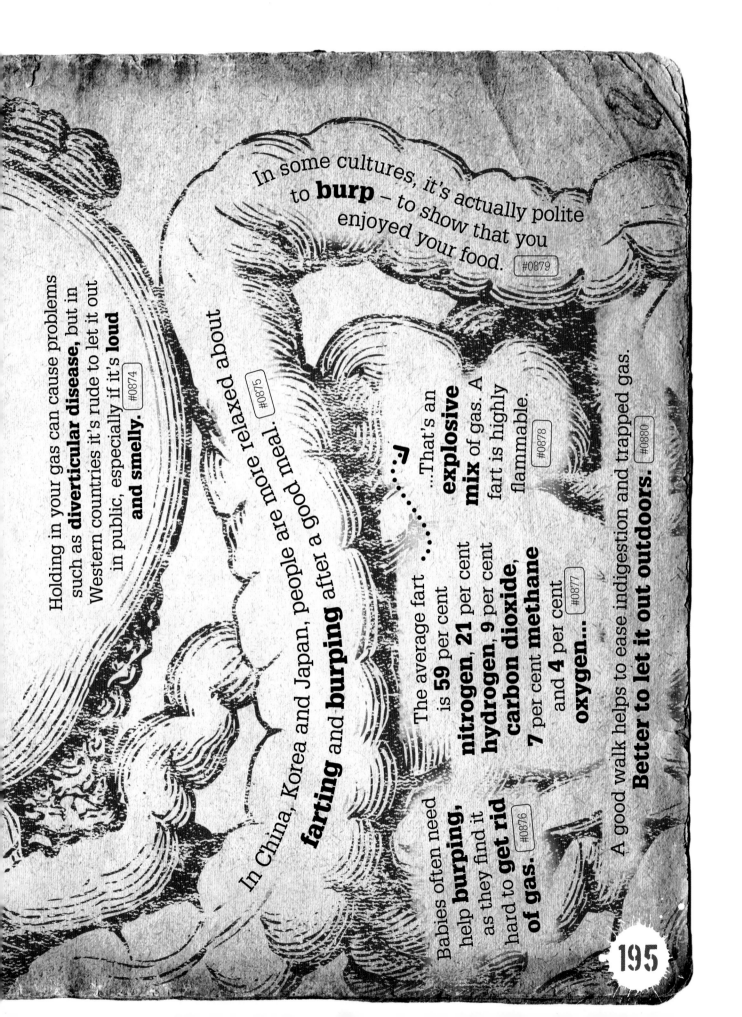

In some cultures, it's actually polite to **burp** – to show that you enjoyed your food. #0879

Holding in your gas can cause problems such as **diverticular disease,** but in Western countries it's rude to let it out in public, especially if it's **loud and smelly.** #0874

In China, Korea and Japan, people are more relaxed about **farting** and **burping** after a good meal. #0875

The average fart is **59** per cent **nitrogen, 21** per cent **hydrogen, 9** per cent **carbon dioxide, 7** per cent **methane** and **4** per cent **oxygen...** #0877

...That's an **explosive mix** of gas. A fart is highly flammable. #0878

Babies often need help **burping,** as they find it hard to **get rid of gas.** #0876

A good walk helps to ease indigestion and trapped gas. **Better to let it out outdoors.** #0880

195

# 9 VITAL VITAMIN Facts

You can get scurvy if you don't eat enough food with vitamin C. Symptoms include **INTERNAL BLEEDING, TEETH FALLING OUT, SWOLLEN GUMS, MADNESS and even death...**

#0881

Sailors on long voyages were prone to **scurvy** and wrongly believed they could avoid it by eating mustard or drinking vinegar.

#0882

In 1520, Portuguese explorer Vasco da Gama **lost 208 of his crew of 220 to scurvy.**

#0883

...Your legs will also get very **swollen** and you'll **have to keep going** to the **TOILET.**

#0884

Scurvy is not common today, but in 2012, a student in the USA contracted the disease. His diet had included **packets of sugar for breakfast and poptarts for lunch.**

#0885

Not getting enough sunlight can affect your body's ability to process **VITAMIN D.** A lack of vitamin D can cause **RICKETS,** a disease in which **bones and muscles become soft and deformed.** #0887

About one third of children under five suffer from **VITAMIN A** deficiency. In extreme cases, it can cause **blindness** or **death.** #0886

## A LACK OF VITAMIN B7

can cause **hair loss, anaemia, tiredness, hallucinations** and **depression.**

#0888

Not eating enough **VITAMIN B12** can cause HYPOCOBALAMINEMIA. Symptoms include **anaemia, swollen stomach,** and **brain and nervous system malfunctions.** #0889

## 11 YUCKY FACTS ABOUT
# FOOD FROM
# HISTORY

### DRINKS

In ancient Egypt, everyone, including children, drank barley beer. It was more like a cloudy, **lumpy soup** than modern beer. #0890

Some ancient Chinese dynasties liked to gulp down **whole snakes** soaked in wine. #0891

### DELICACIES

Roman Emperor Nero treated his guests to several tasty delicacies including **dormice** sprinkled with poppyseed, **cow's udders,** and a **hare** with 'wings' attached to it. #0892

The Aztecs invented chocolate, but they did not add sugar and drank it as a liquid, rather than eating it in its solid form. #0893

# MAINS

The Manchu Han Imperial Feast, a **108-course** banquet in ancient China, included dishes such as **camel's hump**, **bear's paws**, **monkey's brains**, **rhinoceros tails** and **deer tendons**. #0894

It was once common to eat **seagulls**, either baked or in pies. #0895

Medieval plague cures included eating powdered stag's horn, powdered pearls and emeralds – none of which worked. #0896

Henry I of England got ill and eventually died after eating too many lamprey fish. #0897

In 1455, the Count of Anjou, France, served a feast of enormous pies, each containing **a whole deer**, **a duck**, **6 chickens**, **10 pigeons**, **a rabbit** and **26 boiled eggs**. #0898

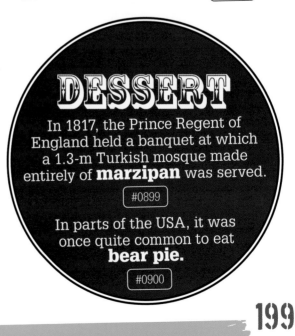

## DESSERT

In 1817, the Prince Regent of England held a banquet at which a 1.3-m Turkish mosque made entirely of **marzipan** was served. #0899

In parts of the USA, it was once quite common to eat **bear pie**. #0900

# 13 CANNIBAL
## FACTS

One of the Aztecs' favourite recipes was a **human stew** called **'tlacatlaolli'**. #0901

In the Middle Ages, some people ground up **ancient Egyptian mummies** to make medicine. #0902

Aztec priests ritually sacrificed enemies, **ripping their hearts out** and **eating their bodies.** #0904

**Hot human blood, distilled brains** and **powdered human heart** have all been used as possible cures for epilepsy. #0903

The Korowai tribe on south-east Papua were cannibals **up until the 1970s,** when they met outsiders for the first time. #0905

'Mellified man' medicine, made from **soaking a human corpse in honey,** was used in Arabia in the 1100s. #0906

The Maori used cannibalism as **a war tactic** – their enemies were terrified at the thought of being **thrown into the cooking pot.** #0907

In the early 20th century, chief Ratu Udre Udre of Fiji is said to have eaten **872 people.** #0908

**'Long pig'** is a cannibal code word for cooked human. #0909

Biting your fingernails is technically **self-cannibalism...** #0910

...As is eating your own hair, which can make **hair-balls** in your stomach... #0911

There is a neurological disease called 'kuru', which can be spread by **eating human flesh.** #0912

...However, **picking your nose** and eating snot is believed to actually **help your immune system.** #0913

201

# **8** facts about ROTTEN FOOD

**Sardinian casu marzu cheese has** maggots put in it on purpose... #0914

...People eat the cheese while the **MAGGOTS** are still alive... #0915

...It gets its special flavour from their poo. #0916

# CIDER-MAKERS
used to add some **MEAT TO THEIR APPLE** and water mixture. As the MEAT ROTTED, it helped the mixture turn to cider... #0917

...The meat was usually **livestock,** but sometimes it came from **rats** that had fallen into the barrels. #0918

202

**Salami** develops a mould around its casing while it's being made. The **mould is often left on** to give it flavour. #0919

In Thailand, you may be served **'stinky meat'** – game animal meat with the maggots left in it. #0920

Some winemakers use **mouldy grapes** to make sweet wines such as **TOKAY OR SAUTERNES.** #0921

203

# 13 facts about SMELLY FOOD

The **smelliest fruit is the durian,** a spiky fruit from south-east Asia. It has been described as **'smelling of stale vomit and sewage'**, but it is supposed to be **VERY TASTY!** #0922

In Korea, STINKY TOFU is a **popular snack,** made of fermented soybeans, vegetables and meat. #0923

**Bombay duck isn't duck.** It's a pongy, dried Indian fish famous for its funny name **(bummalo)** and its awful smell. #0924

**KOPI LUWAK, the world's most expensive coffee,** is made from coffee beans eaten and then pooed out by a small mammal called a **PALM CIVET.** #0925

KIVIAK is an Inuit meal made by stuffing 500 birds into **the body of a seal...** #0926

...It is eaten by making a **HOLE IN THE NECK** and sucking the juices out. #0927

White truffles are **EDIBLE FUNGI** that sell for thousands of pounds per kilogram, despite their strange earthy, mouldy smell. #0928

**Kimchi** is a Korean dish of **fermented, spicy cabbage.** The smell is so powerful that people keep it in a separate fridge. #0929

**Stinking Bishop** has been voted the **smelliest cheese in Britain.** It is soaked in fermented pears to give it its strong smell. #0930

# MISO

is a Japanese paste made from **rice, barley and soybeans.** This mixture is then combined with fungus. #0931

In China, people leave **EGGS TO ROT** for months, or even years, turning the yolks

## DARK GREEN

and smelly, before eating them. #0932

**Surströmming is a Swedish dish** of fermented herring, and is thought to be the **world's smelliest food.** #0933

A **Limburger sandwich** is filled with **raw onion, mustard** and **Limburger cheese,** which smells like BODY ODOUR. #0934

# 11 FACTS ABOUT AWFUL OFFAL

Offal dishes are a popular delicacy in many countries. Offal is the **internal organs and guts of an animal.** #0935

In Brazil, traditional feijoada **(PORK AND BEAN STEW)** sometimes includes the **EARS, FEET** and **TAIL** of a pig. #0936

Animal tongue can be eaten baked, pickled or as slices of cold sandwich meat. #0937

**The rubbery lining** of a cow's stomach is called **tripe,** and can be eaten in different forms depending on which of the three stomach chambers it comes from... #0938

...**Blanket tripe** comes from the first, **honeycomb tripe** from the second, and **book tripe** from the third. #0939

Blood soup is popular in many places around the world. **CZERNINA** is a **Polish soup** made from **DUCK BLOOD** and **HAEJANGGUK** is a **Korean soup** made from **OX BLOOD.**

#0940

**Black pudding** is a blood sausage cooked until it has gone solid.

#0941

Chefs often use caul fat, a thin animal stomach lining, to wrap around meat when cooking. #0942

**HEAD CHEESE,** or brawn, is meat from the head of a pig set in jelly. #0943

Some recipes for meatballs use a pig's liver, lungs and heart.

#0944

**ANIMAL BRAINS** are also eaten around the world. In France, CERVELLE DE VEAU is a dish made from **calf's brains,** while **ox brain fritters are popular in Cuba.**

#0945

207

# 6 FACTS ABOUT STRANGE STOMACH CONTENTS

**In the USA, nearly 5000 OBJECTS** have been **accidentally left inside patients** during surgery in the last 20 years. #0946

'Pica' is the urge to eat non-foods such as CHALK, COAL, DIRT OR SAND. #0947

The most common objects left **inside people** were **sponges,** but **scalpels** and **scissors** have also been left inside. #0948

208

A **man's arm**, a **crocodile head**, **copper wire** and a **pet dog** have all been found inside **SHARKS.** #0949

**A pet dog,** a **football** and a **nappy** have been found in the stomach of an Australian crocodile. #0950

**One grey whale** was found with a stomach **full of rubbish,** including **plastic bags** and golf balls. #0951

209

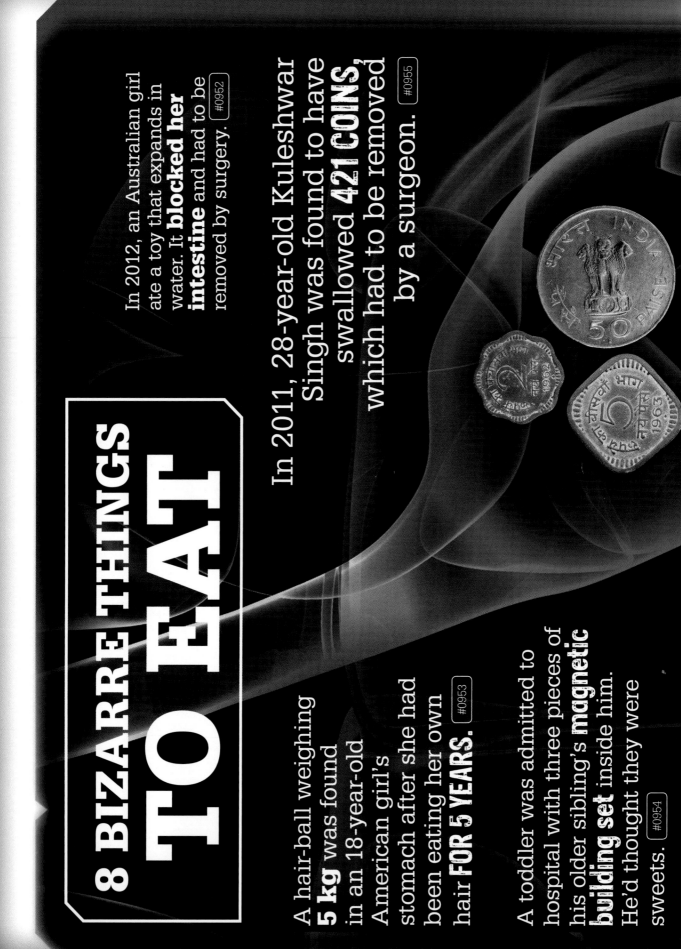

# 8 BIZARRE THINGS TO EAT

In 2012, an Australian girl ate a toy that expands in water. It **blocked her intestine** and had to be removed by surgery. #0952

In 2011, 28-year-old Kuleshwar Singh was found to have swallowed **421 COINS,** which had to be removed by a surgeon. #0955

A hair-ball weighing **5 kg** was found in an 18-year-old American girl's stomach after she had been eating her own hair **FOR 5 YEARS.** #0953

A toddler was admitted to hospital with three pieces of his older sibling's **magnetic building set** inside him. He'd thought they were sweets. #0954

A 32-year-old Israeli woman swallowed **a cockroach** then tried to fish it out with **a fork** but swallowed that, too. #0957

A 19-year-old student accidentally swallowed her **TOOTHBRUSH** while cleaning her tongue. #0959

In 2004, a Californian woman was surprised when she bit into a hot dog and found a **9-mm bullet.** It turned out that she'd already swallowed another one. #0956

A thief swallowed **A DIAMOND RING** just before he was arrested. The jeweller eventually got the ring back after it had been through the thief's digestive system. #0958

# 9 facts about bugs found in food

**THRIPS are tiny insects that hide in fruit and vegetables...** #0960

...Sometimes they are not killed by pesticides so you will probably **swallow a few of them in your dinner.** #0961

Caterpillars live in spinach, AND LAY EGGS ON IT. You will probably find **some larvae on any fresh spinach.** #0962

OREGANO can legally contain up to **1250** INSECT FRAGMENTS PER **10 g.** #0963

There are about **30** aphids (greenfly) in every **100 g** of Brussels sprouts. #0964

There is about **ONE RAT HAIR** **in every** **100 g** of **CHOCOLATE...** #0965

...but there may be up to **FIVE rodent hairs** in every **jar of peanut butter.** #0966

# CINNAMON
can carry up to
# 2 milligrams
**of animal poo per kilogram.**
#0967

There may be up to **19 tiny maggots** and **74 mites** in a **285-g tin of mushrooms.** #0968

# 12 STOMACH-CHURNING FACTS ABOUT FOOD INGREDIENTS

**L-cysteine** is added to processed bread to make the dough stronger. **It can come from bird feathers, pig hair or even human hair.** #0969

CELLULOSE is used to make paper and cotton, but it can also be used as a **fat substitute** or source of fibre in some **processed foods.** #0970

**Carmine is a red colouring used in** CRANBERRY JUICE. It's made from an **acid found in some insects.** #0971

**Castoreum,** an ingredient used to add a **raspberry flavour,** is a **bitter,** smelly brown liquid that comes from a **gland** in a beaver's bottom. #0972

**ISINGLASS** stops beer going cloudy. It is made from dried fish bladders. #0973

**Sheep make a substance called lanolin,** an oil that can be found in many **COSMETICS** and some brands of **CHEWING GUM.**

#0974

Up to **30 per cent of the weight of a frozen chicken** comes from salt water injected into it. #0975

**Vegetable oil with added bromine** is a common ingredient in fizzy drinks. Bromine is also used to stop plastics catching fire. #0976

Shellac, derived from the **female lac bug,** makes a great wood primer. It can also be used to make **SWEETS** or fruit look shiny. #0978

Many cheeses are produced using **rennet,** which comes from **the stomach of a young cow.** #0977

**Silicon dioxide** is the main chemical in **SAND** but is also used to stop powdered food, such as table salt, **GOING LUMPY.** #0980

Ammonia is used on **beef trimmings to kill bacteria and remove fat.** The treated meat **is then added to other beef products.** #0979

# 10 eye-watering SPICE facts

**Moruga Scorpion 2,000,000 SHU**

The Scoville scale measures the strength (hotness) of chilli peppers, or how much they **burn your mouth.**

#0981

**Bell Pepper 0 SHU (Scoville heat unit)**

The hottest chilli pepper ever recorded was a **TRINIDAD MORUGA SCORPION,** which reached over 2 million on the Scoville scale. #0982

Chilli peppers contain **capsaicin, a chemical that irritates human tissue.** If you touch a chilli and then touch anywhere on your body that is sensitive, it will burn. #0983

**Bile is a bitter liquid produced by the liver, which helps the body to DIGEST FAT.** Eating ginger can help increase bile production. #0984

Garlic is used to flavour many foods, but it contains a substance called allyl methyl sulphide, which **makes your breath smell...** #0985

...This garlicky smell can even come out in **YOUR SWEAT.** #0986

The ancient Greeks used mustard paste to **TREAT TOOTHACHE.**

#0987

In 2013, a New Yor[k] restaurant served curry so fiery that che[f] **wore gas mask[s]** to prepare it...

#0[988]

...Their phaal curry registered **1 MILLION** on the Scoville scale...

#0989

...It included the chilli **BHUT NAGA JOLOKIA,** which is also u[sed] to make tear g[as]

#0990

# 10 FACTS ABOUT STRANGE VEGETABLES

If you eat too many carrots, it can cause **carotenaemia** and parts of your skin will turn orange. However, it is not dangerous to your health. #0991

**Cassava** is a root crop that should not be eaten raw because it contains **cyanide**, which can cause paralysis if eaten. #0992

**Nopal** is a vegetable made from the **prickly pear cactus,** with the spiky spines removed. #0993

Beeturia is when your **pee comes out pink** from eating too much beetroot. #0994

**Fiddleheads** are a curly green vegetable eaten in New England, USA. They look like **worms.** #0995

218

Salsify is a root vegetable that **tastes** quite like **oysters**. #0996

Dulse is a **red alga** that hangs from shorelines like seaweed. It is a popular snack in Ireland and Iceland. #0997

In south-east Asia **cha om** is put in omelettes, giving off a **horrid whiff** before it is cooked. #0998

Peter Glazebrook, a grower of **giant vegetables**, grew an **8-kg onion.** #0999

Chinese artichokes look like **little insects,** but are usually pickled and put in salads. #1000

# INDEX

# ACKNOWLEDGEMENTS

**t = top, b = bottom, l = left, r = right, c = centre**

1tl Pdtnc/Dreamstime.com, 1b Eric Issellee/Shutterstock.com, 2 all arlindo71/istockphoto.com, 4tr Dreamstime.com, 4c istockphoto.com, 4b Asier Villafrance/Shutterstock.com, 5tr Milos Luzanin/Shutterstock.com, 5crt sailko/Creative Commons Attribution-Share Alike 3.0, 5crb Plume Photography/Shutterstock.com, 5br p.studio66/Shutterstock.com, 6-7 D. Kucharski K. Kurchaska/Shutterstock.com, 8l Dragon_fang/Dreamstime.com, 9r Nruboc/Dreamstime.com, 10tl sdominick/istockphoto.com, 12 artjazz/Shutterstock.com, 13t Dreamstime.com, 14bl chikapylka/Shutterstock.com, 15c Dreamstime.com, 16tr Shell114/Shutterstock.com, 16cl princessdloft/istockphoto.com, 17tl Eleonora Kolomiyets/Shutterstock.com, 17br gorilla images/Shutterstock.com, 18-19 Shutterstock.com, 19tr tehcheesiang/Shutterstock.com, 20l Dreamstime.com, 21bl Bevan Goldswain/Shutterstock.com, 22-23 Rocky Mountain Laboratories, NIAID, NIH, 24bl Fotosmurf02/Dreamstime.com, 25tr Tatappo/Dreamstime.com, 26-27tc Martan/Shutterstock.com, 27r Dreamstime.com, 29tr Dreamstime.com, 29br lucato/istockphoto.com, 30-31 picsfive/Shutterstock.com, 32l Fotograf77/Dreamstime.com, 33tr istockphoto.com, 35r Monkey Business Images/Shutterstock.com, 36-37 Freddy Thuerig/Shutterstock.com, 38b Emi/Shutterstock.com, 39tr Kurt/Shutterstock.com, 39br Shane White/Shutterstock.com, 40br r.classen/Shutterstock.com, 41tr Carolina Smith/Dreamstime.com, 43bl Mairead/Dreamstime.com, 45tr Galyna Andrushka/Shutterstock.com, 47tr Dreamstime.com, 48tl Darrenp/Shutterstock.com, 49tc istockphoto.com, 50b Dreamstime.com, 51bl nicolas.voisin44/Shutterstock.com, 52bl James H. Robinson/Science Photo Library, 53tc Jubal Harshaw/Shutterstock.com, 54c Griffin024/Dreamstime.com, 54bl SPL, 55tr Aughty/Dreamstime.com, 55br FLPA/Lynwood Chace, 55bl stoykovic/Shutterstock.com, 56-57 istockphoto.com, 56tc Paul Fleet/Dreamstime.com, 56bc Peter Waters/Shutterstock.com, 57tc Xenobug/Dreamstime.com, 57c ex0rzist/Dreamstime.com, 58t Blanscape/Dreamstime.com, 58-59b Clearviewstock/Dreamstime.com, 60tr Pdtrc/Dreamstime.com, 60bl Dan Gerber/Shutterstock.com, 61c Lisa S./Shutterstock.com, 61b Prillfoto/Dreamstime.com, 63b arlindo71/istockphoto.com, 64tr Edd48/Creative Commons Attribution-Share Alike 3.0, 65bl Diane Bray/Creative Commons Attribution-Share Alike 3.0, 65tr NOAA, 66-67 Eris Isselee/Shutterstock.com, 67tr Maksym Boderchuk/Shutterstock.com, 68-69 Everett Collection/Shutterstock.com, 70b Christophe Boisvieux/Corbis, 72-73b Asier Villafranca/Shutterstock.com, 75r Leswrona/Dreamstime.com, 76-77 pzAxe/Shutterstock.com, 76c Cosmin Manci/Shutterstock.com, 82b Maksym Bonderchuk/Shutterstock.com, 83bl Elenathewise/Dreamstime.com, 84bl Lukiyanova Natalia/Shutterstock.com, 84-85b elnavegante/Shutterstock.com, 87b exopixel/Shutterstock.com, 89t Antonio Abignani/Shutterstock.com, 89cr Nicemonkey/Shutterstock.com, 89b Elfim Belousov/Shutterstock.com, 93cl Velazquez77/Shutterstock.com, 94b Bob Thomas/Popperfoto/Getty, 96-97 Igor Lateci/Shutterstock.com, 96bc Baemcr/Dreamstime.com, 98-99 Anatolich/Shutterstock.com, 101b Cathy Keifer/Shutterstock.com, 103t koya979/Shutterstock.com, 103cl Chaoss/Dreamstime.com, 105cr photastic/Shutterstock.com, 106b Ungarf/Dreamstime.com, 107 Milos Luzanin/Shutterstock.com, 109tr cynoclub/Shutterstock.com, 109bl huronphoto/istockphoto.com, 110cr vdeenko/Shutterstock.com, 111tr Didier Descouens/Creative Commons Attribution-Share Alike 3.0, 111cb Dimasobko/Dreamstime.com, 112bl Kkaplin/Dreamstime.com, 113tr Icholakov/Dreasmtime.com, 113br Marafona738/Dreasmtime.com, 115tc okili77/Shutterstock.com, 115bl Stuart Jenner/Shutterstock.com, 116-117 Sergey Nivens/Shutterstock.com, 116cr monticello/Shutterstock.com, 117tc Emley Smith/Shutterstock.com, 117br vnovikov/Shutterstock.com, 118-119 Makson Kabakov/Shutterstock.com, 118br Evgeny Karandanyev/Shutterstock.com, 119bl Alexander Ryanbintov/Shutterstock.com, 120b ollyy/Shutterstock.com, 121tr (iPad) FrankGaertner/Shutterstock.com, 121tr (Google Glass) Tedeytan/Creative Commons Attribution-Share Alike 2.0, 121b Andrey_Popov/Shutterstock.com, 122-123 Phiseksit/Shutterstock.com, 124-125c NASA, 125t Robynrg/Shutterstock.com, 125br Dvmsimages/Dreamstime.com, 126tl Sirophat/Shutterstock.com, 126bl, br, 127 all NASA, 128-129 zhuda/Shutterstock.com, 130-131ODM/Shutterstock.com, 130-131 (leaves) smuay/Shutterstock.com, 131r Arun Roisri/Shutterstock.com, 132br Seleznev Oleg/Shutterstock.com, 132-133c cglade/istockphoto.com, 133bl Nightowiza/Dreamstime.com, 133r Annavee/Shutterstock.com, 134b Olga Dalynenko/Shutterstock.com, 135tr saluha/istockphoto.com, 135cr Artiesky/Shutterstock.com, 135bl Vovashevchuk/Dreamstime.com, 136-137 all Dreamstime.com, 138-139b Dreamstime.com, 139tr Anita Ponne/Shutterstock.com, 140tr nevenm/Shutterstock.com, 140-141b Dennis M. Sabangan/epa/Corbis, 142-143 Robert Adrian Hillman/Shutterstock.com, 144-145 Dreamstime.com, 144-145b Shutterstock.com, 146 rangizzz/Shutterstock.com, 146cl Chaoss/Dreamstime.com, 148-149 all Shutterstock.com, 152b Aero17/Dreamstime.com, 152cl Studiovin/Shutterstock.com, 154bl Michael Rosskothen/Shutterstock.com, 155tr Africa Studio/Shutterstock.com, 155cr Victor Prymachenko/Shutterstock.com, 156b Sailko/Creative Commons Attribution-Share Alike 3.0, 157b Infomages/Shutterstock.com, 158-159 Lena Lir/Shutterstock.com, 160l AFP Getty, 161t Gauravmasand/Dreamstime.com, 162-163 Dreamstime.com, 164 hxdbzxy/Shutterstock.com, 165 Dragana Gerasimoski/Shutterstock.com, 166c Edward Westmacott/Shutterstock.com, 167tr Anniwalz/Dreamstime.com, 167b Getty Images, 168br Fechetm/Dreamstime.com, 171tr Norman Poggon/Shutterstock.com, 171br jadimages/Shutterstock.com, 174tl Hellen Sergeyeva/Shutterstock.com, 175br Ryzhkov Alexandr/Shutterstock.com, 177t xpixel/Shutterstock.com, 177bl Plume Phtography/Shutterstock.com, 178bl mrubic/Shutterstock.com, 178-179 Shutterstock.com, 179tr Planctonvideo/Dreamstime.com, 180l wrangler/Shutterstock.com, 181tr Shutterstock.com, 181b travellight/Shutterstock.com, 182br chlppix/Shutterstock.com, 183tl Everett Collection/Shutterstock.com, 184tl Sarah Marchant/Shutterstock.com, 185b Angonius/Shutterstock.com, 186bl Steve Bower/Shutterstock.com, 188-189 FiledIMAGE/Shutterstock.com, 190bl meunierd/Shutterstock.com, 190-191c Donald Hoen/Creative Commons Attribution 2.0, 191tr Kostov/Shutterstock.com, 191br p.studio66/Shutterstock.com, 192bl kati1313/Shutterstock.com, 193tr Disorderly/Dreamstime.com, 194tl Jinga/Shutterstock.com, 194-195 Shutterstock.com, 197cl Triff/Shutterstock.com, 197br igor.stevanovic/Shutterstock.com, 198bl pick/Shutterstock.com, 199cl bitt24/Shutterstock.com, 199cr erlire74/Shutterstock.com, 200-201 all Shutterstock.com, 202tl Shardan/Creative Commons Attribution-Share Alike 2.5, 203tr gcpics/Shutterstock.com, 203c dabjola/Shutterstock.com, 203b LockStockBob/Shutterstock.com, 204c Eldred Lm/Shutterstock.com, 204b Nordling/Shutterstock.com, 205tr Jiang Hongyan/Shutterstock.com, 205cl margouillat photo/Shutterstock.com, 205bl ArTono/Shutterstock.com, 206tl AnjelikaGR/Shutterstock.com, 207tr de2marco/Shutterstock.com, 207cl Mirabelle Pictures/Shutterstock.com, 208l f9photos/Shutterstock.com, 208cr Noraluca013/Shutterstock.com, 209 pattyphotoart/Shutterstock.com, 210-211 all Shutterstock.com, 212tl Sirikorn Techatabihop/Shutterstock.com, 213br antpkr/Shutterstock.com, 214tr Guzel Strudio/Shutterstock.com, 214bl fotofactory/Shutterstock.com, 214br Tim UR/Shutterstock.com, 215tr Stock Lite/Shutterstock.com, 215c Phil MacDonald/Shutterstock.com, 216tr Swapan Photography/Shutterstock.com, 216bl Andre S/Shutterstock.com, 217t Studio VIN/Shutterstock.com, 217l carlosdelacalle/Shutterstock.com, 218-219 Shutterstock.com, 218cl My Life Graphic/Shutterstock.com, 219tc Robert Taylor/Shutterstock.com, 219cr Piamsak Hansuri/Shutterstock.com

224